The
ates
the
nds

THE WASHINGTON PAPERS

. . . intended to meet the need for an authoritative, yet prompt, public appraisal of the major developments in world affairs.

President, CSIS: David M. Abshire

Series Editor: Walter Laqueur

Director of Publications: Nancy B. Eddy

Managing Editor: Donna R. Spitler

MANUSCRIPT SUBMISSION

The Washington Papers and Praeger Publishers welcome inquiries concerning manuscript submissions. Please include with your inquiry a curriculum vitae, synopsis, table of contents, and estimated manuscript length. Manuscript length must fall between 120 and 200 double-spaced typed pages. All submissions will be peer reviewed. Submissions to *The Washington Papers* should be sent to *The Washington Papers*; The Center for Strategic and International Studies; 1800 K Street NW; Suite 400; Washington, DC 20006. Book proposals should be sent to Praeger Publishers; 90 Post Road West; P.O. Box 5007; Westport, CT 06881.

The United States and the Pacific Islands

John C. Dorrance

Foreword by William J. Crowe, Jr.

Published with the Center for
Strategic and International Studies
Washington, D.C.

Westport, Connecticut
London

DU
30
.D68
1992
Sept 2002
A BO 2332

Library of Congress Cataloging-in-Publication Data

Dorrance, John C.
    The United States and the Pacific Islands / John C. Dorrance.
       p.   cm. — (The Washington papers, ISSN 0278-937X ; 158)
    Includes bibliographical references (p.   ) and index.
    ISBN 0-275-94471-9 (cloth). — ISBN 0-275-94472-7 (paper)
    1. Oceania — Relations — United States. 2. United States —
Relations — Oceania. 3. Oceania — History. I. Title. II. Series.
DU30.D68   1992   92-19951
327.730182′3 — dc20

British Library Cataloging-in-Publication data is available.

Library of Congress Catalog Card Number: 92-19951
ISBN: 0-275-94471-9 (cloth)
       0-275-94472-7 (paper)

First published in 1992

Praeger Publishers, 88 Post Road West, Westport, CT 06881
An imprint of Greenwood Publishing Group, Inc.

Printed in the United States of America

Contents

Foreword

I met John Dorrance in the fall of 1970 when I reported to the Office of Micronesia Status Negotiations. I was consistently amazed at his prolific writing and jokingly referred to him as "the fastest typewriter in the West." John had been selected as the political adviser to the High Commissioner of the Trust Territory and participated from the outset in the negotiations to terminate the Trust. Over the next few years he served in Australia, Fiji, and Papua New Guinea. By the time of his death in 1991 he was considered one of the nation's leading authorities on the Pacific Islands.

This current work, which was John's last effort, gives us an unprecedented overview of this often neglected but nonetheless important part of the world. Americans in particular are linked through military history, trade, trustee responsibilities, fiscal, and governmental ties to this region. Although the trusteeship is on the brink of disappearing, Washington's obligations – security, political, economic – to the people of those islands remain strong.

Decision makers seized with policy responsibilities regarding the Western Pacific will find this book a "must." John treats U.S. policy involvement in detail and in particular traces the history of the trusteeship. Likewise, he weaves in the influence of other external powers with emphasis on Japan and the Soviet Union. The result is a comprehensive look at the various influences that have shaped the islands and produced their contemporary problems. He concludes with a thoughtful analysis of where the future is leading. Of interest to American scholars and academics will be John's recommendations regarding Washington's role in relations with the various island states.

Only someone with John's knowledge – not just of the area's history but of the island peoples, institutions, and cultures – could have written such a human and sensitive treatment of this complex subject. Its high quality is a fitting tribute to a bona fide scholar and statesman who spent a great deal of his life working on behalf of the Pacific Islands.

William J. Crowe, Jr.
Admiral, U.S. Navy (Ret.)

August 1992

About the Author

John C. Dorrance, an independent foreign affairs consultant and analyst until his death in 1991, specialized in the affairs of Australia, New Zealand, and the Pacific islands during much of his career in the U.S. Foreign Service (1956–1989). Assignments abroad included Australia (twice), Fiji, Micronesia, and Papua New Guinea, and also Vietnam, Jamaica, and Germany. Assignments in the Department of State involved U.S. policy planning, international security issues, UN and East Asian affairs, the Pacific islands, Australia, and New Zealand. In 1988–1989 he was a senior fellow at the Institute for National Strategic Studies of the National Defense University, Washington, D.C. Earlier, in 1978–1979, he served on the faculty of the National War College. Mr. Dorrance authored several books and numerous journal articles on U.S. interests and policies in the Pacific area.

Prefatory Note

John Dorrance completed this study at the start of 1991. Illness, and later his death, prevented him from working any further on the manuscript. No effort has been made to rewrite his work. It stands on its own merits as a record, as an interpretation by a seasoned observer-participant, and indeed as a sensible, informed set of policy prescriptions that have not been overtaken by time.

Nor has any effort been made to bring statistical material up to date. The figures used by John Dorrance are still valid insofar as they reflect trends or relativities that continue to apply. The same can be said for his recommendations.

Adjustments to the text were needed, however, to reflect the passage of time. CSIS and Praeger are grateful to Professor Henry Albinski, director of the Australia–New Zealand Studies Center at Pennsylvania State University, for undertaking this task and for assisting the editorial staff during the production of this volume.

Summary

Although the Pacific islands were front-page news during the 1941–1945 Pacific war, today they are seldom in the American consciousness – except as a perception of Micheneresque tropical paradises. But the islands – 10,000 strong and scattered over nearly one-fifth of the earth's surface – still straddle or remain close to the sea- and air lanes that link the United States with Australia and Asia and carry nearly one-half of U.S. foreign trade. New political interests also exist with the recent emergence of a new galaxy of independent Pacific island states, extension of U.S. sovereignty to other Pacific islands, and new defense responsibilities in several states linked to the United States by "free association."

The region's continuing political evolution ensures that the United States can no longer afford policies that have been characterized as benign neglect. The Pacific islands, highly aid dependent and uniquely vulnerable to external influences, have experienced insurrections, military coups, secessionist rebellion, political assassinations, Soviet inroads, and Libyan mischief-making. Ethnic conflict and developmental problems also threaten democratic institutions and the region's stability – and thus some basic U.S. interest. Other threats to the latter include high levels of anti-

xv

nuclear sentiment, conflicts between some U.S. policies and regional environmental concerns, and remaining decolonization issues. There also are pressures for change within the U.S. territories, especially Guam and the Commonwealth of the Northern Mariana Islands. The latter suffers the birthing pains of the first U.S. territorial acquisition since the Virgin Islands in 1917.

The region warrants higher levels of U.S. attention from yet another perspective. Despite the above problems, the Pacific islands' record in the areas of human rights and democratic government remains vastly superior to that of other Third World regions. This enviable record, if it is to survive and be further strengthened, does require tangible U.S. and other Western support.

From these perspectives, John Dorrance has analyzed the Pacific islands policy environment, the interests and roles of other external powers active within the region, U.S. regional interests and objectives, challenges to those interests, and optimum policy strategies. He points out that Washington's tendency toward inattention interspersed by occasional reactive diplomacy is a strategy that is not only ineffective, but also can be costly in the long term. It has already occasioned massive erosion of the reservoir of regional good will that existed after World War II. He concludes that the region fortunately remains a relatively low-threat environment where a small investment in attention, sensitivity, and resources can yield major dividends for U.S. interests.

Dorrance drew heavily on his exposure to the region and related issues as an area specialist in the Department of State's Foreign Service. His research included extensive background conversations with U.S., Australian, French, New Zealand, and island state officials and scholars in 1989 and 1990. He also had a three-week program of dialogue with Soviet officials and Asia-Pacific academic specialists in mid-1990 as a guest of the Institute of Oriental Studies of the Soviet Academy of Sciences, Moscow. The resulting chapter on Soviet regional interests and policies is uniquely definitive.

This volume offers an exceptionally authoritative and comprehensive assessment of U.S. interests in and policy toward a poorly understood region. That, and the accompanying thorough exploration of the regional policy environment, and of issues that face the United States, will be of value to scholars interested in the region, but above all to policymakers and practitioners in Washington and other Western capitals. The passage of time and unfolding of events have demonstrated the accuracy of Dorrance's previous analytical work in this area. The U.S. foreign affairs community thus would do well to heed his conclusions and recommendations in this most recent effort.

The
United States
and the
Pacific Islands

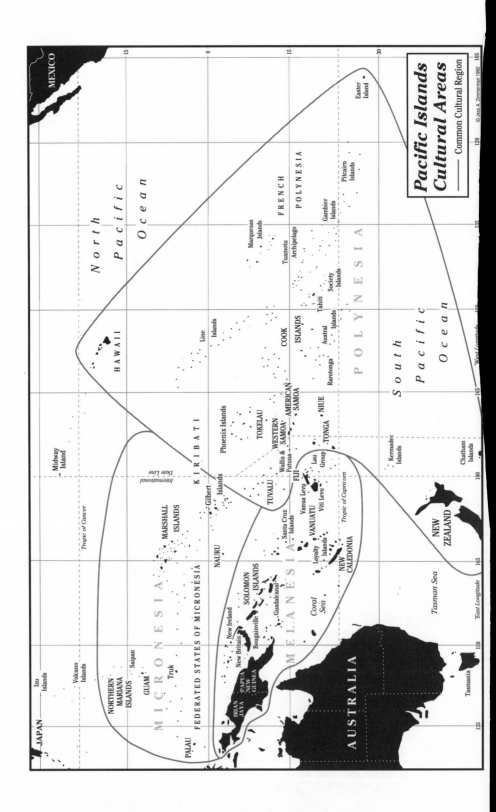

Pacific Islands Cultural Areas

—— Common Cultural Region

© Jess A. Zimmerman 1992

1

Oceania: The Strategic Environment

When Western media, governments, and publics comment on the extraordinary evolution of the Pacific Basin, or the Asia-Pacific region, they almost always focus on the rim nations. Little thought or comment is directed at Oceania — the "in-between" Pacific islands. Yet until recently these islands were the region's essential stepping stones of both commerce and war. The evolution of transport, communications, and defense technology has largely eliminated the latter aspects of strategic importance. But the region's political evolution, new technologies, possible (if improbable) future conflict scenarios, and the U.S. territorial presence ensure the region's continued strategic relevance to the United States.

Most Americans regard the Pacific islands, except when they served as World War II battlegrounds, as a Micheneresque, tranquil backwater where modest U.S. interests require little attention. Until recently, nearly all the islands of the North Pacific were under U.S. political control while those in the South Pacific (except American Samoa) were colonies of allies — Australia, Great Britain, France, and New Zealand. But decolonization, begun in 1962, has transformed the Pacific political map. Today there are

1

thirteen independent or quasi-independent Pacific island states; more are likely to emerge in the 1990s.

Several of these new island states have chosen a political status unique to Oceania—that of sovereign self-governing states in free association with external powers. Two of them—the Federated States of Micronesia and the Republic of the Marshall Islands—have such a relationship with the United States. Each controls its own internal and foreign affairs but has vested defense responsibility in the United States. A third such relationship, one between Palau and the United States, has yet to be implemented. Another island group, the Northern Mariana Islands, has entered into a commonwealth relationship with the United States—the first U.S. territorial acquisition since the Virgin Islands in 1917.

Despite technological and regional political change, one fact underlies U.S. regional interests and concerns: the Pacific islands are astride or contiguous to critical trans-Pacific air and sea routes. These routes carry nearly one-half of the foreign trade of the United States and also link the United States with five of its seven security alliances. These two factors alone provide reason enough to deny military access to potential adversaries.

New security interests have evolved from changing defense technology or political change elsewhere. A major example is the importance of the Kwajalein Missile Range facility in the Marshall Islands to intercontinental ballistic missile (ICBM) testing and to the development of the Strategic Defense Initiative (SDI). Guam's importance to U.S. Western Pacific deployments has risen since the failed negotiations over the renewal of American basing rights in the Philippines. Palau and the Northern Mariana Islands in the recent past were seen somewhat as partial "fallback options" should the United States lose access to bases in the Philippines, but any such adjustments are currently unlikely.

The region also dominates the strategic approaches to a

key ally—Australia. Australia's defense policies and force structure assume that any direct threat will be through or from these islands and Indonesia. New Zealand's defense forces are similarly oriented toward potential regional threats. France asserts that access to its nuclear test site in French Polynesia remains essential for maintenance and modernization of its independent nuclear forces. Its suspension of nuclear tests in 1992 was promised only for that calendar year, to be reconsidered afterward.

A relatively new Western interest is political: the importance of pro-Western democratic regional governments in supporting the political, social, and economic aspirations of their people, and the resulting stability that serves security interests. Western economic interests remain relatively minor with notable exceptions: investment in the mineral resources of Papua New Guinea, the region's rich tuna resource, and the potential for exploiting seabed mineral resources.

Tranquil images of the region are deceptive. Most island states have little or no potential for economic development that promises future self-sufficiency; they are probably permanently dependent on aid to maintain even minimum services, social and otherwise, essential to the welfare of their populations and political stability. At the political level, the absence of progress toward decolonization of the French territories and delays in that process in Palau have occasioned political violence in these areas, including insurrection in New Caledonia. Racial conflict in Fiji led to two military coups in 1987 and the suspension of democratic institutions in that key regional state.

In recent years the region also has variously witnessed political assassinations and other terrorism, chronic political instability in some states, and military incursions by Indonesian forces into the region's largest state, Papua New Guinea. The latter also suffers from centrifugal separatist forces, including an armed rebellion on copper-rich Bougainville Island.

TABLE 1
Basic Data on the Pacific Islands

State/Territory	Current Political Status	Previous Colonial Links	Land Area (sq. miles)	EEZ Sea Area (sq. miles)	1990 Population (estimation)
American Samoa	U.S. territory (1899)	None	77	150,579	41,840
Cook Islands	Free association with New Zealand (1965)	New Zealand, Britain	94	706,563	18,187
Federated States of Micronesia	Free association with United States (1986)	U.S., Japan, Germany, Spain	271	1,149,806	104,937
Fiji	Independent (1970)	Britain	7,126	498,069	759,567
French Polynesia	French territory (1843)	None	1,273	1,942,083	190,181
Guam	U.S. territory (1898)	Spain	211	84,170	141,039
Kiribati	Independent (1979)	Britain	266	1,370,655	70,012
Marshall Islands	Free association with United States (1986)	U.S., Japan, Germany	70	1,370,655	43,417
Nauru	Independent (1968)	Australia, Germany	8	123,552	9,202
New Caledonia	French territory (1853)	None	7,450	671,814	153,215
Niue	Free association with New Zealand (1974)	New Zealand, Britain	101	150,579	2,019

4

Northern Mariana Islands	U.S. commonwealth territory (1986)	Japan, Germany, Spain	184	300,000	22,719
Palau (Belau)	U.S. trust territory (1947)	Japan, Germany, Spain	178	242,857	14,310
Papua New Guinea	Independent (1975)	Australia, Britain, Germany	180,274	1,204,632	3,822,875
Pitcairn Islands	British colony (1895)	None	18	309	56
Solomon Islands	Independent (1978)	Britain	11,126	517,374	335,082
Tokelau Islands	New Zealand territory (1925)	Britain	4	111,969	1,700
Tonga	Independent (1970)	Britain	272	270,270	101,313
Tuvalu	Independent (1978)	Britain	10	347,490	9,136
Vanuatu	Independent (1980)	Britain, France[a]	4,633	262,548	165,006
Wallis and Futuna	French territory (1887)	None	99	115,830	14,910
Western Samoa	Independent (1962)	New Zealand, Germany	1,144	46,332	186,031
Totals			214,889	11,638,136	6,189,754

[a]Prior to independence, Vanuatu was administered jointly by Britain and France as the New Hebrides Condominium.

Source: Central Intelligence Agency, The World Fact Book, 1990 (Washington, D.C.: CIA, 1990).

Frustration arising from such economic and political problems, generational leadership change, the emergence of widespread and emotional antinuclear sentiment, and the region's recent interaction with Indonesian, Japanese, Libyan, Chinese, the former Soviet, and other external influences – some positive and some negative – have forever altered the political environment.

The prospect today is for more rather than fewer developments that will threaten regional, U.S., and allied interests. That trend is paralleled by an ongoing erosion of goodwill toward the United States brought on in large measure by Washington's inattention and by policies that conflict with regional state interests. The suspension of the New Zealand-United States leg of the Australia-New Zealand-United States (ANZUS) alliance has further complicated the region's political and security environment.

Current U.S. policies toward the region, although for the most part pointed in the right direction, are inadequate in the face of new challenges to old interests. In general, the region now requires a higher level of U.S. involvement in and commitment to its development, both political and economic.

The Land, the Sea, the People

Oceania is simultaneously gargantuan and minuscule. Its 22 states and territories embrace 10,000 islands scattered over about 20 percent of the earth's surface, although the islands have a land area of only 219,889 square miles (roughly the size of Texas). The bulk of this land area is found in one country – Papua New Guinea. In contrast to lilliputian land areas, the Pacific islands' exclusive economic zones (EEZs) blanket 11.6 million square miles of the Pacific. One of the smallest states, Kiribati, has an EEZ equal in size to all of Western Europe.

Western geographers more than 150 years ago categorized the region ethnically and culturally as Melanesia (black islands), Micronesia (small islands), and Polynesia (many islands). Micronesia today embraces Guam, the Northern Marianas, Palau, the Caroline Islands (Yap, Truk, Pohnpei, and Kosrae) that form the Federated States of Micronesia, the Marshall Islands, Kiribati (formerly the Gilbert Islands), and Nauru.

Polynesia (aside from islands on the extreme perimeter not covered in this study – Easter Island, Hawaii, and New Zealand) embraces American Samoa, the Cook Islands, Fiji (culturally), French Polynesia, Niue, Pitcairn Islands, the Tokelau Islands, Tonga, Tuvalu (formerly the Ellice Islands), Wallis and Futuna, and Western Samoa. Fiji geographically and ethnically joins Melanesia's New Caledonia, Papua New Guinea, the Solomons, and Vanuatu (formerly the New Hebrides).

Oceania's three subregions have geographies as diverse as their cultures. The Micronesian islands of the North Pacific are mainly atolls, a few raised atolls, and scattered volcanic high islands. Few have economic resources of any significance, except the resources in the surrounding seas. The South and Central Pacific Polynesian subregion possesses more volcanic islands but is equally bereft of land-based resources. Micronesia and Polynesia together lay claim to most of the region's islands, states, and territories, but to only about 7 percent of its land mass, which is concentrated in the continental and volcanic islands of Melanesia northeast of Australia. These islands contain most of the region's mineral and agricultural resources.

Geographic diversity translates into major differences in national scale: from Papua New Guinea with a land mass roughly equal to that of Spain to tiny Nauru with only eight square miles, but paradoxically one of the world's highest per capita national incomes. The high income flows from phosphate deposits that will be depleted in the 1990s.

Most island states are frequently subjected to natural disasters, primarily hurricanes but also tidal waves and volcanic activity in some areas. If pessimistic global warming and greenhouse-effect predictions are accurate, some atoll nations (for example, Kiribati, the Marshall Islands, and Tuvalu) may be submerged by the surrounding seas in the twenty-first century.

The region's population of 6.2 million also offers dramatic contrasts, ranging from Papua New Guinea's 3.8 million, many only a generation or two removed from the stone age, to the few dozen descendants of the *Bounty* mutineers who inhabit Britain's last Pacific islands colony – the Pitcairn Islands. More than half the region's population is under age 16, and population growth rates are among the world's highest. Only the safety valve of emigration from some Polynesian and Micronesian states (mainly to Australia, New Zealand, and the United States) currently holds population growth rates within manageable proportions. Except in the Melanesian states with literacy rates as low as 13 percent, Pacific islanders are well educated by developing world standards. A relatively high proportion has received some secondary education, and literacy rates are generally well above 75 percent.

Island state and territory populations, with some major exceptions in Polynesia and Micronesia, tend to be ethnically, culturally, and linguistically heterogeneous. The region's 1,200 languages comprise about 25 percent of the world's recognized language groups. About 800 languages are spoken in Papua New Guinea alone. An extreme example of ethnic and cultural pluralism is New Caledonia, where French settlers, together with Polynesian, Vietnamese, and Indonesian immigrants, form that territory's majority. Descendants of indentured Indian labor were the largest ethnic group in Fiji until recently. Since the 1987 coups, differential demographic growth patterns and Indian emigration have ensured ethnic Fijians a plurality in that country. Communities of Europeans, Chinese, and other islanders form a separate but important minority. Most other regional states and territories also have small but economically important Chinese and "European" (white) communities. The latter are mainly Australians and New Zealanders in the South Pacific and Americans in the North Pacific.

Decolonization

Despite a lack of exploitable resources, Oceania experienced a remarkably complex colonial history. At various times between the sixteenth and twentieth centuries, the Spanish, Germans, Dutch, and Japanese had a colonial presence. Some island areas of Micronesia have seen more than 300 years of foreign rule and four successive colonial masters. But the major scramble for Pacific colonies took place in the late nineteenth and early twentieth centuries by Australia, Britain, France, New Zealand, and the United States.

The United States entered the colonial era at the turn of the century when it acquired American Samoa, Guam, and Hawaii. After World War II, U.S. political presence increased in the region with Japan's transfer to the United States of the Northern Mariana (mainly Saipan and Tinian), Caroline (Palau, Yap, Truk, Pohnpei, and Kosrae), and Marshall Islands. Formerly governed by Japan under a League of Nations Mandate, they became the Trust Territory of the Pacific Islands, under a U.S. obligation to guide them toward self-government or independence.

The region's colonial era was generally benign compared with the colonial periods of Africa and Asia. Traditional cultures were relatively less disturbed, except for the introduction of Christianity. Only two colonial powers actively promoted settlement of their Pacific colonies – Japan in Micronesia before World War II and France in New Caledonia.

Late to be colonized, except for the Spanish areas of Micronesia, Oceania also was among the last regions to enter the decolonization cycle. The latter began in 1962 when Western Samoa achieved independence from New Zealand. It peaked in the 1970s and continued in the 1980s, but decolonization is likely to be completed only in the 1990s when the future political status of French Polynesia, New Caledonia, and Palau is resolved.

Unlike African and Asian experiences, the Pacific islands' transitions to independence or self-government were generally orderly and nonviolent. Most initiatives for political change came from the administering powers rather than from indigenous pressures. By 1986 such initiatives had resulted in nine independent and four self-governing states. With the exception of Vanuatu, which joined the Non-Aligned Movement, all transfers of power from metropolitan authorities were to pro-Western governments. (Papua New Guinea joined the Non-Aligned Movement, but apparently for pragmatic reasons flowing from its bilateral relationship with Indonesia; it maintains an essentially pro-Western foreign policy.)

The remaining colonial presence consists of the following: France and the United States, each with three territories; New Zealand in the Tokelau Islands; and Britain in Pitcairn. France is being pressured to decolonize in New Caledonia and French Polynesia, and the United States is experiencing pressure in Palau.

Political and Cultural Characteristics

The major success story of decolonization in the Pacific islands has been the blending of Western democratic parliamentary institutions and values with those of traditional cultures into governmental systems that ensure, with some exceptions, levels of democracy and human rights unmatched elsewhere in the Third World. Conservative traditional values in most states, a consensus approach to decision making, a strong sense of communal obligation, and cultural restraints on conflict and confrontation in human relations (except in Melanesia) together promote moderation and pragmatism, as well as resistance to radical change or ideologies. These tendencies are reinforced by the strong religious orientation of island societies; all are devoutly Christian to an exceptional degree. Exceptions are the Melanesian states, particularly Papua New Guinea, where conflict, confrontation, and overt competition for power, wealth, and leadership are major elements of traditional cultures. Some of these latter characteristics also apply to Palau in Micronesia.

Although political parties exist in most areas, few have any ideological content or mass following; they tend to be shifting coalitions built around individual political leaders or linked to traditional geographic and cultural divisions and rivalries. Exceptions include parties in New Caledonia and French Polynesia, with their focus on the issue of ties with France; those in Fiji, which focus on ethnic politics and the issue of tradition versus modernization; and parties in Vanuatu, which do have a mass base and some distinctive ideological content. Fiji's Labor party, and the opposition coalition grouping of which it is a part, also has favored some nonalignment in foreign affairs and nuclear-free policies similar to those of New Zealand. A Labor party established in the Solomon Islands reflected a leftist bias; it was led by a Moscow-trained labor leader who had links with Soviet international front organizations.

As elsewhere, certain leadership and cultural characteristics are important considerations for an external state's relations with the region. The following paragraphs describe the most critical; although not necessarily unique to the area, these characteristics are unique in their degree of relative importance.

Decision making at all levels normally is a slow and deliberate consensus process. Intuitively cautious about change and new directions, and uncomfortable with the divisions and conflict inherent to decisions by vote (except in parts of Melanesia), islanders tend to avoid action on important questions until the majority fully comprehends and supports a course of action. These traits are generally counterproductive to any hard-line pursuit of controversial objectives or effort to play one group of leaders off against another. Patience, gentle persuasion, and careful cultivation of key opinion leaders are by far the most effective diplomatic tactics.

As elsewhere in the developing world, most decision making of national or international importance is limited to a few elites who tend to lead rather than follow any public opinion that may exist. This factor, coupled with a tradition of communicating orally and settling issues through face-to-face dialogue, makes high-level personal contact critical between island leaders and U.S. officials on issues important to the United States.

Everywhere there is a spiritual attachment to the land and the surrounding seas unparalleled in Western or most other societies. Clan or kin groups identify with and are identified by clearly delineated traditional attachments. The living generation is in effect the guardian or trustee of land for preceding and successor generations. Loss of land and its resources can be culturally and politically devastating in island societies. Deprivation of traditional land holdings fuels the current separatist rebellion on Bougainville Island in Papua New Guinea and Kanak pressures for independence in New Caledonia. The perceived threat to ethnic Fijian land was one concern motivating Fiji's 1987 military coups against a predominantly Indian-supported government. U.S. military use or potential future use of island land has posed the single most difficult issue between the United States and the Micronesian states of the North Pacific.

The region is experiencing accelerating political change that tends to erode traditional decision-making processes and social restraints and affects attitudes toward relations with the United States and other traditional ties. Urbanization, particularly among the young, education, and exposure to a variety of such other new influences as an expanding media are key factors in the current transition to what might be called modernization.

Education in particular is rapidly expanding the numbers of elites involved in decision making and exposing a younger generation to values and concepts at odds with the traditional conservatism of the first generation of postcolonial political leaders. Monetization of island economies and decreasing reliance on subsistence agriculture is also driving change, as is the increasing importance of trade unions in labor-management relationships and as a political force.

The rate of change varies between island states. As a generalization, however, younger political and other elites are far better educated than their predecessors, less attached to traditional values and assumptions, more prone to experimentation in international relations, often skeptical or even resentful of traditional foreign ties, sometimes more ideological in their approach to both domestic and international issues, and in some instances skeptical about the relevance of Western political values and institutions. By developing-world standards, however, most emerging political elites remain remarkably conservative, pragmatic, and committed to democratic principles and free enterprise systems.

All the island states are hypersensitive about their sovereignty. Their smallness, vulnerability, and aid dependency make them quick to perceive threats or slights and prone to accept conspiratorial interpretations of events beyond their control. One consequence has been a degree of paranoia regarding mythical Central Intelligence Agency (CIA) and other U.S. activities. It has been promoted by U.S., Australian, and New Zealand leftists and peace groups and inadequately addressed by the United States.

Economic Characteristics

Although the Pacific island states are among the world's least developed and least resource-endowed, a few do possess some important natural resources.

• Most of the world's tuna supply is taken from the region. Some EEZ seabeds also possess significant but unexploited mineralization, mainly manganese nodules.

• Forty percent of the world's known nickel reserves are in New Caledonia, which also has rich but only partly exploited cobalt, iron, and chrome deposits.

• Papua New Guinea possesses massive gold and copper deposits and is likely to become the world's third largest

gold producer in the 1990s (after the Commonwealth of Independent States and South Africa). It also has large but as
yet unexploited petroleum and natural gas fields and indi-
cations of bauxite, zinc, coal, and iron. Some of these same
minerals also are present, but not yet exploited, in the Solomon Islands and Vanuatu.

• Nauru is the primary source of phosphate for Australia, Japan, and New Zealand.

The island states nonetheless share a number of fea-
tures that perpetuate economic fragility and, on a per capita basis, the world's highest levels of aid dependency. Except for Papua New Guinea and Fiji, all suffer from small
land mass and population with resulting inability to
produce a range of goods and services normal to larger
economies. Because of such diseconomies of scale, governments must provide most basic services and are thus the
largest employers. Government activity in the smaller
states accounts for 50 to 95 percent of gross domestic product (GDP). Remittances (returns of earnings) from island
state citizens working in Australia, New Zealand, and the
United States often are a major source of foreign exchange,
40 percent in the case of Western Samoa. A majority of the
populations of most states continues to rely largely on subsistence agriculture. Education and urbanization are weak-
ening that traditional sector and consequently increasing
pressure on scarce opportunities in the money economy,
wage-earning sector.

The resources of Micronesia and Polynesia are generally
limited to the ubiquitous coconut palm and its products, a
few other tropical agricultural products, timber in a few
places, tuna in the surrounding seas, and tourism in some
areas. The Melanesian states possess most of the foregoing
resources, as well as significant timber resources and commercial agriculture (coffee and tea in Papua New Guinea,
rice in the Solomon Islands, and sugar in Fiji).

Aside from external aid, the economies of most states
thus depend on income from a narrow range of primary

TABLE 2
Basic Economic Data on the Pacific Islands

| State/Territory | Gross Domestic Product (US$) | | | Aid Receipts, 1988 (US$ 000) |
	Year	Millions	Per Capita	
American Samoa	1985	187.5	5,282	48,100
Cook Islands	1988	40.0	2,200	18,200
Federated States of Micronesia	1989 (GNP)	150.0	1,500	103,400
Fiji	1989	1,320.0	1,750	42,500
French Polynesia	1987	2,055.8	12,047	265,860*
Guam	1988 (GNP)	1,000.0	7,675	106,300
Kiribati	1989	34.0	500	17,200
Marshall Islands	1989	63.0	1,500	48,300
Nauru	1989 (GNP)	90.0	10,000	0
New Caledonia	1987	810.3	5,353	78,169*
Niue	1987	3.0	1,072	7,300
Northern Marianas	1987	245.6	12,343	52,200
Palau (Belau)	1986	31.6	2,260	27,400
Papua New Guinea	1988	3,260.0	890	355,900
Pitcairn Islands		N.A.	N.A.	300*
Solomon Islands	1988	156.0	500	36,700
Tokelau Islands	1988	1.4	800	1,928*
Tonga	1989	86.0	850	18,100
Tuvalu	1987	120.0	820	25,300
Vanuatu	1987	120.0	424	13,400
Wallis and Futuna	1985	6.7	484	20,082*
Western Samoa	1989	112.0	615	27,100

*1987 data.
Sources: For GDP data, see *South Pacific Economies Statistical Summary*, no. 11, 1987 (Noumea, New Caledonia: South Pacific Commission, 1990); and Central Intelligence Agency, *World Fact Book, 1990*. For aid data, see data and sources in table 3, this volume.

products. All are exceptionally vulnerable to global market forces over which they have no influence. All energy sources, nearly all finished products, and a high proportion of foodstuffs are imported at high cost from outside the region — a primary cause of island country inflation. Almost all states have negative foreign trade balances.

Fiji, French Polynesia, Vanuatu, the Northern Marianas, Palau, New Caledonia, the Cook Islands, and Western Samoa do have a significant tourism industry with potential for further development. Some states also have pursued such innovative and occasionally dubious sources of foreign exchange as merchant marine "flag of convenience" arrangements (principally the Marshall Islands and Vanuatu), Cayman Islands–style international banking (principally the Marshall Islands, Vanuatu, and Nauru), and marketing of passports (mainly Tonga and the Marshall Islands). There have been allegations that some of the above banking systems have been used by drug cartels for money laundering and by con artists for investment scams.

U.S. and French military activities yield economic resources for a few areas. Expenditures and employment are associated with France's nuclear test center in French Polynesia, with the U.S. Kwajalein Missile Range facility in the Marshall Islands, and with the U.S. bases on Guam.

Small industry has been developed only in Fiji, Papua New Guinea, and to some degree Tonga. Aside from Papua New Guinea, the other Melanesian states, and Fiji, population size, distance from markets, and few commercially exploitable resources limit foreign investment. Foreign investment is encouraged everywhere, however. Most investment has traditionally come from Australia and New Zealand in the South Pacific and the United States in the North Pacific. In recent years, Japan has also become a major source of investment capital, particularly in tourism, fisheries, timber, and mineral resource development. The highest levels of foreign investment are in Papua New Guinea and Fiji. The region's banks, most regional air services, much small industry, most large commercial trading ventures, and the media are to a great degree foreign owned.

Although populations continue to grow and place increasing pressures on limited resources, few island states in recent years have had increases in gross domestic product. Most are depending increasingly on aid. The per capita GDP of many independent or self-governing states is well under $900, rising at the start of the 1990s above that level only in Fiji, the Cook Islands, Nauru, Niue, the Marshall Islands, and the Federated States of Micronesia. It is also well above that amount in the French and U.S. territories, but only because of massive subsidies. Income and GDP data in most cases also are inflated by the salaries and expenditures of large communities of expatriates employed by governments and the private sector.

Island State Viability, Stability, and Fragility

Until recently, the relative tranquility of the region was largely due to its isolation from global ideological trends and pressures, superpower competition, and modernization. The absence of alternatives in most areas ensured unquestioning acceptance of subsistence life-styles, low levels of social and other services, and traditional leadership authority. Mass education, travel, urban drift, monetization of economies, enhanced internal and external communications, and the influences of new external forces together ensure rising economic and social expectations, varying levels of political frustration, and other challenges to stability. The foregoing factors, coupled with a drift to towns away from village life and traditional subsistence agriculture and unemployment rates as high as 80 percent, have already eroded traditional social restraints, as manifested in the major law and order problems of Papua New Guinea, high rates of alcoholism everywhere, and some of the world's highest youth suicide rates.

Aside from aid dependency, there are seven major threats to island state viability and stability: ethnic pluralism; cultural and linguistic pluralism coupled with centrifugal separatist forces; modernization versus tradition; leadership rivalry; rising economic and social expectations; the fragility or weakness of governmental institutions; and vulnerability to external mischief makers.

Fiji and New Caledonia are beset with problems of ethnic pluralism. As discussed in chapter 3, the indigenous Kanaks have become a minority in New Caledonia where French settlers control most of the land as well as the political and economic life. Cycles of violence ensued as the Kanaks sought independence and were resisted by French and other non-Kanak ethnic groups. The 1988 accords between the French government and the various communities in New Caledonia now provide some hope for peaceful resolution.

In Fiji, descendants of indentured Indian labor were the largest ethnic group until recently. This group has dominated small business, services, the vital sugar industry, the labor movement, and most professions. Ethnic Fijians retained control of their land and dominated government until 1987 when a coalition of Indians and Fijians placed in office an Indian-dominated government. Military coups followed and displaced Fiji's last democratically elected government with one determined to impose a constitution perpetuating ethnic Fijian political control and traditional leadership authority. Although no blood was shed, the seeds of future instability and ethnic violence exist. Large arms shipments of uncertain origins were uncovered in Fiji, and the Indian community became embittered – as were some modernized Fijians who rejected traditional authority patterns.

The United States, Australia, and New Zealand publicly condemned the coups; they temporarily suspended development assistance to, and (over the longer term) defense cooperation with, Fiji.[1] Fiji has responded with efforts to establish new trade, investment, and political ties with several Asian nations and France. France has been generous with military and development assistance in return for anticipated tolerance of French nuclear testing and territorial policies.

With the exception of educated elites, Pacific islanders have little sense of nationhood. Much of Papua New Guinea's population, as an extreme example, was only a generation or two removed from the Stone Age when that country became independent in 1975. There is little sense of identification beyond small language and kin groups. Tribal warfare was common and continues sporadically. National politics are characterized by revolving-door parliamentary governments where shifting political loyalties, often purchased, and competition for power and wealth inhibit any government's ability to govern and plan on a long-term basis. Corruption is commonplace, even at the highest levels of government. Urban drift, the related breakdown of cultural restraints, and massive unemployment in Papua New Guinea's towns have led to endemic problems of law and order, requiring martial law to be imposed at times. A poorly disciplined military has in certain respects proved to be part of, rather than a solution to, the law and order problem.

Disputes over allocating Papua New Guinea's wealth and national power have made separatist movements a constant threat, particularly on Bougainville Island where the world's largest copper mine has provided 45 percent of national export earnings and 17 percent of government revenues. Resentment over the loss of control of hereditary lands, the transfer of most mining revenues to the central government, and concern for environmental damage led to a separatist rebellion that forced the mine to close in mid-1989. The outcome, though now unclear, may be a precedent for other provinces that possess major gold, oil, and other resources.

The classic conflict between the forces of modernization and traditional authority is in some degree a problem everywhere in the Pacific, but potentially greatest in the Kingdom of Tonga where all political power and most wealth has until recently been reserved to the king and a few nobles. Despite some reforms, the political caste system minimizes the potential for political, economic, or social advancement for commoners, except through emigration to New Zealand or elsewhere. Further pressures for reform cannot be discounted and, if not addressed, could bring instability to the kingdom. The same problem exists to some degree in Western Samoa, but there it is offset by flexibility in distributing the traditional titles that are the key to advancement in that society and by some movement toward universal suffrage; Western Samoan voters narrowly approved a referendum on universal suffrage in October 1990. There also is growing resentment of traditional leadership authority and associated corruption in the Marshall Islands.

Political rivalry is not unique to the Pacific islands, but it has traumatically affected some island areas. Two cases in point are Vanuatu and Palau. Factional strife in Vanuatu has led to violence and constitutional crises. Traditional clan and other rivalries in Palau underlie differences over the political future and nuclear issues in that last remnant of the U.S. Trust Territory of the Pacific Islands. These rivalries are the root cause of considerable violence, including the assassination of Palau's first president.

Modernization has raised economic expectations everywhere, and no island state government (except Nauru's) can adequately satisfy them with domestic resources. Economic development, social services, and adequate levels of employment thus depend on foreign aid and investment, and in many states, there are few incentives to attract such aid.

Perhaps a problem rather than a threat, nearly all island government institutions suffer a lack of well-trained staff. Education is bringing improvement, but for years to come most island governments and major elements of the private sector will have to employ extensive and expensive contract expatriate staff, primarily Australians and New Zealanders. There are some 15,000 expatriates in Papua New Guinea alone.

Small and vulnerable island states also have provided fertile ground for con artists and other external mischief makers. A few years ago a Texas real estate promoter absconded with Tuvalu's cash reserves. The conservative Phoenix Foundation of Hawaii invested in real estate in Vanuatu just before independence in 1980 and, following that event, promoted (apparently in collusion with France) a separatist insurrection. The newly independent state had to call on the Australian-supported military forces of Papua New Guinea to restore peace and national unity. At another level, the Libyans in the past financed and provided paramilitary training to factions in Vanuatu and New Caledonia. Misguided and ill-informed external peace groups have confused the issues involved in Palau's future political status and have needlessly complicated the resolution process.

Considerable evidence indicates that international drug cartels, including major Japanese crime syndicates, are now operating in the region, apparently in search of safe havens for funds, money-laundering facilities, and transit points for drugs.

Future Prospects

Although prediction is at best an exercise in informed guesswork, current trends suggest the following developments in the 1990s:

1. The decolonization cycle will be completed. Palau is likely to enter into some form of free association with the United States by mid-decade (see chapter 5). New Caledonia will achieve either independence or some form of free association with France by 1998 (chapter 3). French Polynesia also will become more autonomous. The U.S. territories will retain their political links with the United States, but Guam almost certainly will move to some form of commonwealth status within the next few years. American Samoa may also seek a higher level of self-government (chapter 5).

2. The Tokelau Islands, Pitcairn Islands, and Wallis and Futuna will remain dependencies on New Zealand, Great Britain, and France, respectively.

3. Tonga almost certainly will face major pressures to accelerate reform and to modernize its political structure. The passing of the now elderly king probably will provide the catalyst for change. Western Samoa and the Marshall Islands will experience similar pressures to a lesser degree. All three probably will adjust slowly but adequately and without bloodshed.

4. As Fiji's ethnic Fijian population moves from plurality to majority in the next generation, and as forces for modernization weaken the authority of traditional leaders, Fiji may revert to a political system providing something closer to equal political status for all ethnic communities, but with continuing constitutional safeguards for ethnic Fijian control of land. Ideological forces already present may also contribute toward less conservative but not radical government.

5. Papua New Guinea's chronic political instability and periodic secessionist movements will continue, but it is hoped they will fall short of breaking up that state. A level of autonomy verging on independence, or even independence itself, cannot be ruled out for Bougainville Island and the other islands of the North Solomons Province. Either development could establish a major negative political and economic precedent for the rest of that troubled state. There also is the related potential for a military or police coup or for other undermining of that nation's fragile democratic institutions. These problems in nation building may make it increasingly difficult to attract the foreign investment capital essential to the development of Papua New Guinea's rich resource base.

6. Generational change and other forces for modernization will continue to weaken traditional values and political processes and in some areas bring more ideology to politics. By developing world standards, however, most island states

probably will remain moderate, democratic, and free enter-prise-oriented.

For the Western powers with major interests in the re-gion – particularly Australia, France, New Zealand, and the United States – many of these forces or trends are not easily subject to direct influence or management, except in one major way. The level and character of development assis-tance and other support will continue to be key to the inter-nal political stability of most island states.

2

Foreign Affairs, Security, and Regionalism

Most South Pacific states have little choice but to give first priority to relations with Australia and New Zealand. These two countries are accepted as regional powers, major trading partners, and key sources of development assistance and private investment capital. Often they are also effective advocates of island state interests in Washington, Moscow, and Tokyo and in various international organizations. But their pervasive presence and influence are often resented, driving regional state efforts to diversify external ties. Fiji's government in particular has resented Canberra's and Wellington's frequent public criticism of its failure to restore democracy, including equal political rights for all ethnic communities. One consequence has been a major Fijian effort to establish new economic and political links with the Association of Southeast Asian Nations (ASEAN) and other Asian states.

Relations with Japan are of growing importance to the region; Tokyo—now the second largest South Pacific aid donor after Australia—is becoming the major source of private investment capital. The island countries attach high importance to their relationships with the United States, but they are often frustrated by a lack of reciprocal interest. In the North Pacific, states in free association with the

United States give first priority to that relationship. For economic reasons, they also attach high importance to their relations with Japan.

With the exception of Vanuatu's traditional distrust but recently improved relations with France, all island states have close ties with their former colonial administrators. All of the former Australian, British, and New Zealand colonies, except for Fiji, also retain British Commonwealth links. (Fiji's Commonwealth links ended with the 1987 military coups.) Only Fiji, Papua New Guinea, the Solomon Islands, Vanuatu, and Western Samoa have joined the United Nations. Except for nonaligned Vanuatu, all the states have voting records generally more supportive of Western positions than can be found elsewhere in the developing world.

Although the island states traditionally tended to be suspicious of Soviet regional interests and activities, most established diplomatic relations with the Soviet Union. Only Papua New Guinea, however, accepted a resident Soviet diplomatic mission. The Soviet Union's successor states have had neither the incentive nor the resources to seek regional diplomatic representation for themselves. Regional perceptions of the new Russia and of the closing of the cold war have overcome past concerns about Soviet regional initiatives.

Although Papua New Guinea is not an ASEAN member, its size and geographic proximity to Indonesia and Southeast Asia have led to an interest in the region and observer status in ASEAN. (A recent effort to obtain full ASEAN membership was rebuffed.) An insurrection in Irian Jaya, along Indonesia's and Papua New Guinea's common land border, and related Indonesian military action also lend particular importance to that bilateral relationship (chapter 7). Several other island states, particularly Fiji, have also developed links with ASEAN states in an effort to diversify diplomatic and economic relationships. Most island states have trade and investment ties with Taiwan; a few maintain diplomatic relations with Taiwan rather than the People's Republic of China. Most maintain relationships with China (see chapter 7). Except for Vanuatu, all island states have adopted essentially pro-West foreign policies. In the past several years, even Vanuatu has moved toward more moderate foreign policies and closer relations with the United States.

The limited resources of the island states generally constrain their foreign affairs activities to major issues directly affecting their interests, particularly those touching on their economic development and regional resources, regional decolonization, and the regional environment. A major exception is Fiji's traditional participation in Middle East peacekeeping forces.

Regional State Security
Perceptions and Concerns

Although not in the strictest sense an issue, the differing perceptions that regional states and external powers have of their respective security interests may cause friction. Most external powers active within the region perceive their primary interests as strategic and political. This point particularly applies to Australia, New Zealand, and the United States, but also to Japan and France.

Island governments understand and mostly accept fundamental Western regional strategic interests and related security and political objectives, except for French nuclear testing. Nonetheless, aside from Papua New Guinea, which has had problems along its land border with Indonesia, and possibly the Solomons, which have experienced friction with Papua New Guinea as a result of Papua New Guinea's efforts to overcome the rebellion in Bougainville, no island state perceives any potential external military threat beyond the possibility of incidental involvement in a broader conflict. For this reason, most regional governments (particularly in Polynesia and Micronesia) have supported Western strategies for deterring conflict and their requirements within the region. Most regional states also welcomed the security umbrella of the ANZUS alliance and were concerned by the breakdown of the U.S.–New Zealand leg of that alliance.

The Melanesian states sometimes articulated the view that superpower rivalry within the region could have involved them unnecessarily in any future East-West conflict. This view was particularly strong in Vanuatu. Until recently, Vanuatu tried to balance East-West contact and influence with an array of relationships unique to the region (for example, relations with Cuba, Libya, North Korea, and Vietnam) and relatively balanced relations with the United States and the Soviet Union.

In contrast to Western geopolitical concerns, island state security concerns relate to economic insecurity; inadequate development assistance and increasing aid dependency with a resulting perception of limits on political freedom of action; high levels of unemployment and other social problems in urban centers; violations of sovereignty (for example, marine resource piracy); insensitivity by other countries to regional interests (for example, U.S. failure to adhere to the South Pacific Nuclear Free Zone (SPNFZ)–Treaty of Rarotonga protocols and Japanese driftnet fishing); assumed environmental contamination by French nuclear testing; and past French colonial policies. A major new concern is the potentially devastating impact that global warming could have on the survival of several island nations.

Internal political instability in some areas could reach proportions that external military intervention would be requested. The precedent exists in Vanuatu, where Papua New Guinea forces, with Australian transport and logistics support, intervened to support the government against an armed insurrection shortly after independence in 1980.

Only four states — Fiji, Papua New Guinea, Tonga, and Vanuatu — maintain military or paramilitary forces. Fiji's force, the largest, peaked in 1990–1991 at about 5,000 (but is now declining); many have extensive experience in Middle East peacekeeping operations. Papua New Guinea's army numbers about 3,350. Tonga's small defense force numbers only 350, while Vanuatu's Mobile Force is a 270-strong paramilitary unit. Australia and New Zealand have major defense cooperation programs with many South Pacific states, although those with Fiji were suspended following the 1987 military coups. Fiji developed new defense links with France, Indonesia, Malaysia, and Pakistan and managed to maintain long-standing ties to UK forces. Papua New Guinea is seeking to augment its traditional sources of defense programs, Malaysia being the foremost new connection. Although U.S. defense links with regional defense forces have been limited, they have expanded modestly in the past several years in exercises, training, and equipment transfers. They are mainly with Papua New Guinea; those with Fiji have been suspended.

There are no security alliances between island states and, aside from the defense responsibilities of the United States and New Zealand for the island states in free association with them, no formal security commitments by external powers other than arrangements to consult in the event of a threat. The most important of the latter is the arrangement between Australia and Papua New Guinea.

Regionalism and Regional Institutions

Limited size and resources, along with economies of scale and many common national interests, have encouraged the development in Oceania of regional cooperation mechanisms unique in their cohesion, influence, and effectiveness. The origins of Pacific islands' regionalism were a Western colonial initiative: the 1947 Canberra Agreement establishing the South Pacific Commission (SPC) to coordinate or promote development and resource-related research in the region's Australian, British, Dutch, French, New Zealand, and U.S. territories. The SPC today is the only regional organization providing full participation to all twenty-two island states and territories, to Australia and New Zealand,

and to the remaining colonial powers – Britain, France, and the United States. The SPC's secretariat in Noumea, New Caledonia, promotes, funds, and coordinates a broad range of technical and development assistance projects, particularly in the smaller states and territories. Its policies and programs are determined by an annual South Pacific conference where independent and self-governing island states, dependent territories, and external powers have an equal voice and vote. Primary funding is from Australia, France, New Zealand, and the United States.

Objections to SPC restraints on discussing political issues, and a perception that it is dominated by the external powers, led to the establishment of the South Pacific Forum in 1971. The forum now includes all independent and self-governing island states (that is, those in free association with New Zealand and the United States), plus Australia and New Zealand. The fifteen forum heads of government meet annually and decide by consensus on regional political, economic, social, and environmental issues. In 1973 the South Pacific Forum secretariat was established in Suva, Fiji (originally as the South Pacific Bureau for Economic Cooperation), to serve as the forum's secretariat and to promote and coordinate development assistance within the region. In 1989, the forum initiated a postforum meeting dialogue with senior representatives of key nonforum states (Britain, Canada, France, Japan, and the United States) on issues of mutual interest. The dialogue is patterned on ASEAN's annual postministerial meetings with key nonmembers.

From its outset, the forum has addressed the full range of regional concerns, except those involving the internal affairs of members. Examples include initiatives in the United Nations and elsewhere on decolonization of New Caledonia; establishment of the South Pacific Nuclear Free Zone and related pressures on French nuclear testing in French Polynesia; cooperation with other international organizations (for example, the Asian Development Bank, the World Bank, the United Nations Development Program, and the European Community) to promote development assistance to the region; promotion of free trade arrangements; establishment of specialized regional organizations such as the Forum Fisheries Agency and a regional shipping line; and coordinated implementation of the Law of the Sea regime. Current topics of greatest concern are environmental and fisheries issues.

For most of the smaller island states, the forum provides the most effective means to press foreign policy objectives. For all, it provides the synergistic effect of a single major voice heard in distant capitals. The consensus approach to decision making also ensures moderation in forum activities.

Other major regional organizations include the Forum Fisheries Agency (headquartered in Honiara, Solomon Islands), which seeks to manage and conserve the region's fisheries resource and often acts as an agent for individual members. The U.S. regional fisheries treaty discussed in chapter 3 was negotiated with that agency. Yet another organization is the regional Forum Line that provides a subsidized regional shipping service, in some instances to areas that otherwise would not be served. The South Pacific Applied Geoscience Commission, or SPAGO (originally the Committee for the Coordination of Joint Prospecting for Mineral Resources in South Pacific Offshore Areas), headquartered in Suva, Fiji, is responsible for managing regional marine seabed research. Australia, New Zealand, and the United States cooperate closely with SPAGO. The Soviets offered research support, but were rebuffed.

Many regional organizations—particularly the South Pacific Commission, the South Pacific Forum, and the Forum Fisheries Agency—also serve as a conduit for official development assistance to the region, especially U.S. assistance because, until recently, Washington preferred to sponsor regional projects rather than multiple bilateral aid programs.

Cracks are occurring, however, in regional cohesion and cooperation, arising from subregional political and leadership rivalries and jealousies as well as from differing per-spectives on some political issues. The Micronesian and Polynesian states tend to be more conservative than the larger Melanesian states and have resented the regional leadership aspirations of Fiji and Papua New Guinea. They also argue that the South Pacific Forum has tended to cater to the needs of the larger island states. The Melanesian states have formed the "Spearhead Group" that has tended to press more radical positions on decolonization and nucle-ar issues.

The Melanesians also have argued that the South Pacif-ic Commission is a remnant of colonialism that competes with the South Pacific Forum for resources. In the past, they have argued for abolishing the commission and estab-lishing a single regional organization that would not give full voice to Britain, France, the United States, and the remaining dependent territories.

The smaller Polynesian and Micronesian states oppose abolishing the commission, arguing that its projects are often best tailored to the needs of small states. The South Pacific Forum in 1988 established, with the agreement of other major regional organizations, the South Pacific Or-ganization Coordinating Committee. That mechanism ap-pears, at least for the moment, to have defused the "single regional organization" issue.

The Melanesian Spearhead Group has become less united and outspoken. The Solomons have quarreled with Papua New Guinea's handling of the Bougainville dispute, while Vanuatu's earlier, more experimental foreign policy approach has weakened.

Future Prospects

Growing frustration with current levels of aid and other dependence on a narrow range of traditional Western links will accelerate current trends toward experimenting with new international ties. Regional political initiatives and rhetoric largely intended just to demonstrate independence may increase. To some degree this situation may explain Papua New Guinea's decisions to accept an embassy and a controversial fisheries agreement with what used to be the Soviet Union and to establish diplomatic relations with Cuba. Some drift toward nonalignment may also occur, but probably not to the point of actions that might threaten access to major traditional Western sources of aid and investment. Regional security will continue to focus on internal rather than external concerns, given current prospects for higher levels of political instability or volatility and the falling away of great power rivalries.

These problems may be compounded by a leveling off of, even reduction in, development assistance flows owing to a mix of external factors. Traditional donors are increasingly faced with competing domestic and foreign priorities (for example, U.S. and European donors have new programs in Eastern Europe to consider, as well as aid to the Soviet Union's successor states). Ironically, improving East-West relations may ill-serve regional state interests. The generosity of Western donors to some degree had been driven by the need to counter a perceived but now dissolved Soviet threat. "The Russians are coming" syndrome can no longer be a catalyst for regional aid.

Despite centrifugal forces, the economies of scale offered by regional institutions in the pooling of small-state resources suggest that the role of these institutions will continue to expand. For the smaller states in particular, the importance of these regional mechanisms may grow as a means of competing for finite global aid resources and for coping with the range of external power activities within the region.

3

Regional Issues and Challenges

At what points do the region's interests and activities intersect with and sometimes conflict with those of outside powers? The most important areas include the sources, magnitude, distribution patterns, and character of development assistance; global warming, nuclear concerns, and other environmental issues; remaining decolonization problems; and threats to regional marine resources.

Development Assistance and Dependency

The Pacific islands are the most aid dependent of all global regions, especially in the area of budget-support grants. Although comprehensive current data on official development assistance (ODA) flows are elusive, assistance exceeds $1,000 per capita in several island states and most dependent territories. With few exceptions, it is essential for national survival. An extreme example is the Marshall Islands where more than 90 percent of government revenues derive directly or indirectly from U.S. grants and other U.S. payments. Development assistance in some cases exceeds GDP.

Estimates of total ODA flows to the region vary dramatically, according to whether dependent territories are included.[2] With the latter included, total ODA to the Pacific islands was about $1.6 billion in 1990, but only about half of that total went to independent and self-governing states. (These estimates are higher than those shown in tables 3 and 4; they reflect recent increases in Japanese, French, and EC aid to the region.)

The above estimates highlight a major imbalance in regional aid flows: the U.S. and French dependent territories, with only 9 percent of the region's population, receive nearly half of regional external financial assistance. A related distortion is that the North Pacific islands (Guam, the Northern Marianas, Palau, the Federated States of Micronesia, and the Marshall Islands), with only 5 percent of the region's population, receive (primarily from the United States) about 24 percent of the region's external financial assistance.

The primary donors in 1988, by order of magnitude of ODA to other than dependent territories, were Australia, the United States, Japan, the World Bank (IBRD), the European Community (EC), New Zealand, the UN Development Program (UNDP), the Asian Development Bank (ADB), Great Britain, France, the Federal Republic of Germany, and Canada. The People's Republic of China and Taiwan are also donors, but no reliable current data are available. If the two North Pacific Micronesian states in free association with the United States are excluded from these calculations, U.S. aid to island states in the South Pacific has trailed Great Britain's and in 1988 was about 3 percent of total flows to that subregion.

Patterns of major ODA flows generally relate to past colonial associations or to the donor's perceptions of strategic and political interests. The United States has focused on the North Pacific; Australia on Papua New Guinea (about 84 percent of Australian regional ODA) and other nearby Melanesian states; New Zealand on the Cook Islands, Niue, and Western Samoa; Great Britain on its former colonies; and France on its territories, Fiji, and the Polynesian states. Japan contributes ODA ($93 million in 1989) to nearly all island states either directly or through regional organizations; it is Western Samoa's major aid source.

The EC's Lome Convention arrangement also is increasingly important; $250 million in development assistance was committed to the region for five years beginning in 1991. Of equal importance, the exports of participating South Pacific states and territories have preferential access to EC markets, sometimes at subsidized prices.

From an island state perspective, the above patterns warrant concern. The states see themselves as overdependent on a narrow range of past colonial ties. That perception in turn makes them worry about continuing undue levels of influence and about assumed limitations on their freedom of political action. For these reasons alone, most island states have sought diversified ODA sources as well as private investment and export trade opportunities.

An obvious problem, particularly for the smaller states, has been that they are staffed by small bureaucracies ill equipped to solicit or manage development assistance. This problem, together with the overhead costs of managing several small bilateral ODA programs, has led some donors (particularly the United States in the South Pacific) to channel considerable aid to regional organization projects (for example, those of the South Pacific Forum, the South Pacific Commission, the University of the South Pacific, and the Forum Fisheries Agency) and to projects of private voluntary groups. The regional/multilateral approach, though cost-effective, has a major problem. ODA administered through these channels rarely serves the political objectives of the donor and is widely resented by island governments as a slight to their sovereignty.

Island states dependent on aid for both budget support and infrastructure development face a particularly difficult problem. Uncertainty about future revenue levels makes reliable planning almost impossible. Tuvalu, one of the smallest states, has initiated an innovative solution: the Tuvalu Trust Fund. Donors have been asked to make a major one-

TABLE 3
Official Development Assistance (ODA): Recipients and Major Sources
(1988 data except as noted)

State	ODA (US$ millions)	Per Capita ODA (US$)	Major Sources
1. Independent and Self-Governing States			
Cook Islands	$18.2	$1,011	France, New Zealand
Federated States of Micronesia	103.4	1,202	United States
Fiji	42.5	59	Japan, Australia, New Zealand, IBRD, UK
Kiribati	17.2	259	Japan, UK, Australia, New Zealand, EEC
Marshall Islands	48.3	731	United States
Niue	7.3	2,531	New Zealand
Papua New Guinea	335.9	92	Australia, Japan, EEC, ADB, UK, UNDP
Solomon Islands	36.7	124	Australia, Japan, UK, EEC, UNDP
Tonga	18.1	182	Australia, Japan, New Zealand, EEC, UNDP
Tuvalu	13.4	1,585	UK, New Zealand, Australia
Vanuatu	25.3	164	Australia, UK, Japan, New Zealand
Western Samoa	27.1	152	Japan, Australia, EEC, New Zealand
Subtotal	$693.4	$133	

2. Dependent Territories

American Samoa	$48.1	$1,284	United States
French Polynesia (1987)	265.9	1,504	France
Guam	106.3	830	United States
New Caledonia (1987)	78.2	509	France
Northern Marianas	52.2	2,610	United States
Palau	27.4	2,030	United States
Pitcairn Islands (1987)	0.3	2,980	UK
Tokelau Islands (1987)	1.9	1,205	New Zealand
Wallis and Futuna (1987)	20.1	1,366	France
Subtotal	$600.4	$1,144	

3. Regional Institutions and Projects (1987 data)

Subtotal	$55.0	$10	Australia, UNDP, EEC, United States, New Zealand, France
Total ODA	$1,358.8	$237	United States, France, Australia, Japan, EEC, IBRD, New Zealand, UK

Note: For purposes of this table, official development assistance (ODA) is defined as including budget support grants and grants to dependent territories. Totals for 1988 for each category of ODA include some 1986 and 1987 data that have been projected without change. ODA sources are listed in rough order of magnitude of their contributions. Data do not include contributions from smaller donors – e.g., Germany, Canada, Taiwan, and the People's Republic of China. These contributions total at least another $50 million. Data for the Federated States of Micronesia and the Marshall Islands also do not include ODA from Japan – probably about $20 million.

Sources: U.S. Congress, House Committee on Foreign Affairs, *United States Interests in the South Pacific,* Hearing before the Subcommittee on Asia and Pacific Affairs, 101st Cong., 1st sess. (July 27, 1989); *South Pacific Economies Statistical Summary,* no. 11, 1987 (Noumea, New Caledonia: South Pacific Commission, 1990); the U.S. Census Bureau; the U.S. Agency for International Development; and the U.S. Department of State.

TABLE 4
Official Development Assistance (ODA): Major Donors
(US$ millions in 1988, except as noted)

Donor	ODA to Self-Governing & Independent States & Regional Projects	ODA to Dependent Territories	Totals
Australia	$296.9		$296.9
France	13.5	$362.3 (1987)	375.8
Japan	70.0		70.0
New Zealand	31.8	1.9 (1987)	33.7
United Kingdom	25.1	0.3	25.4
United States	176.6	234.0	410.6
Asian Development Bank	27.5		27.5
European Community	34.2 (1986)		34.2
World Bank (IBRD)	43.9		43.9
UN Development Program	30.8		30.8
Total	$750.3	$598.5	$1,348.8

Note: For purposes of this table, ODA is defined as including budget support grants and grants to dependent territories. Totals for 1988 include some 1986 and 1987 data that have been projected without change. There were in fact significant increases in these categories. Data do not include contributions from smaller donors – e.g., Germany, Canada, Taiwan, and the People's Republic of China. These and other contributions total at least another $50 million.

Sources: As cited for table 3.

time capital contribution to the fund. Interest earned is channeled into the recurring budget. At the end of 1989, the fund's capitalization value was about $33 million; interest earnings covered one-quarter of Tuvalu's budget. Major donors have included Australia, Great Britain, Japan, and New Zealand.

Perceptions among donor nations of relative need are a problem for the region as it competes for an adequate share of global ODA resources. Except for some parts of Melanesia, the regional environment is perceived (except for frequent natural disasters) as relatively gentle. Famine is unknown, and high levels of malnutrition, disease, and infant mortality are relatively rare in most areas other than the Melanesian states and Kiribati, where they are high.

A further perception problem relates to regional per capita GDP and income data. Both are relatively high compared with other Third World regions, but they are grossly distorted by the salaries, allowances, and expenditures of thousands of expatriate staff providing skills not locally available. Ironically, the need to import essential human resources restricts access to aid needed to develop domestic human resources. The problem especially applies to Papua New Guinea, the Solomons, and Vanuatu, a subregion where literacy rates range from an abysmal 13 percent to 32 percent.

The Environment

Environmental concerns loom larger in the political consciousness of Pacific islanders than in any other Third World region. The fragile ecosystem makes some nations highly concerned about their survivability in the face of global warming and the greenhouse effect. Many islanders have believed that the region's most important resource – the seas that surround the islands – is threatened by French nuclear testing in French Polynesia. Other perceived threats have included tendencies by some industrialized nations to view the region as a potential site for the disposal of nuclear and toxic wastes and, most recently by the United States, for the storage and destruction of chemical weaponry.

Global Warming and the Greenhouse Effect

The region's major environmental concerns today are global warming and the greenhouse effect. Although the data involved and the consequent predictions of rising sea levels are currently disputed, there is growing global acceptance of the assumption that, absent corrective measures by the major industrialized nations, global warming ultimately will affect sea levels. In a region where several nations are only a few feet above sea level, rising sea levels would be devastating. There already are projections of sufficient change in the twenty-first century to require the evacuation of the entire populations of the Marshall Islands, Kiribati, and Tuvalu, plus those of the atolls of other island states and territories. Such evacuations could affect at least one-fifth of all Pacific islanders, as well as those nations that would have to accept transplanted populations.

Most industrialized nations are seeking adoption of international conventions and domestic legislation that will restrict carbon dioxide and other industrial emissions assumed to cause global warming. The United States has tended to be the major exception; Washington has argued that evidence has been insufficient to support the more serious global-warming predictions and thus massive new environmental legislation. Caught in a recession, the United States now finds it politically difficult to force new, environmentally driven costs onto domestic industry, or to devote large sums to helping Third World nations improve their own environmental conditions.

The U.S. position has unsettled island state governments, particularly because the United States produces about 22 percent of the world's carbon dioxide output. Global warming now parallels the issue of French nuclear testing in the degree of emotional concern it elicits, most of which is directed at the United States. It was the single most contentious issue discussed at a 1990 Honolulu summit meeting between President Bush and regional heads of government.

*Nuclear Issues and the South
Pacific Nuclear Free Zone*

Nuclear testing is another widespread, highly emotional environmental issue with side effects that directly affect major U.S. security interests. Aversion to nuclear power brought on establishment of the South Pacific Nuclear Free Zone, suspension of the ANZUS alliance relationship between New Zealand and the United States, periodic threats to U.S. Navy port access elsewhere in the region, and a political stalemate in efforts to resolve the issue of Palau's future relationship with the United States.

The origins of the Pacific nuclear-free movement to some degree were U.S. nuclear testing in the Marshall Islands from 1946 to 1958 at Johnston Atoll and Christmas Island from 1958 to 1962, and British testing on Christmas Island and in Australia during the 1950s and early 1960s. The conclusion of U.S. and British nuclear testing in the Pacific in 1962, well before a significant political consciousness emerged in the Pacific islands, probably would have consigned that testing to a historical footnote if not for the unfortunate consequences of the 1954 "Bravo" test at Bikini Atoll. An unanticipated change in wind directions subjected several hundred Marshallese on distant atolls to fallout. Consequent radiation sickness, increases in leukemia rates, and genetic defects in children born since have been given publicity throughout the Pacific. U.S. recognition of its responsibility has included millions of dollars in compensation and massive but largely unsuccessful efforts to clean up the contaminated test sites.

The primary catalyst for regional antinuclear emotions was, however, commencement of French nuclear testing at Moruroa Atoll in French Polynesia in 1966; the Bravo mishap received little regional attention before that testing and subsequently was publicized primarily to generate opposition to French testing (but also to generate pressure for compensation of its victims). There were no nuclear-free movements in the island-country region until 1970 when the regional ATOM (Against Nuclear Tests on Moruroa) Committee was formed in Fiji. That group evolved into the Movement for an Independent and Nuclear-Free Pacific – a loose coalition of church and political leaders, women's groups, academics, trade unionists, environmentalists, and peace groups. The movement embraces not only the Pacific islands but also Australia and New Zealand; individuals and nongovernmental groups in the latter nations have provided much of its finance and leadership. Other sources of support have included peace groups in Japan, Canada, and the United States, the Pacific Trade Union Community (which featured a strong leftist bias and was formed to promote a nuclear-free Pacific), the World Council of Churches, the World Peace Council, the Congress of International Cooperation and Disarmament, and the World Federation of Trade Unions. The latter three organizations were Soviet fronts.

The nuclear-testing issue also has an important anticolonial dimension. Regional leaders and the antinuclear movement argue that French testing has been imposed on a colonized Pacific people who have not participated in relevant Paris decision making. More recently, however, French testing has been viewed primarily as an environmental threat, principally to the sole significant resource of many regional states – the seas that surround them. Although only scattered evidence supports allegations that French nuclear testing has already seriously contaminated some nearby areas, there is concern that protracted underground testing ultimately may breach the fragile reef structure of the test site, resulting in a massive release of radioactivity into the surrounding sea. The fact that France has already shifted some tests to a nearby second atoll site, Fangataufa, suggested that Paris acknowledges that risk. The 1992 French decision to place tests in abeyance for the remainder of the year was probably influenced more by domestic political than by external considerations.

Regional opposition to French nuclear testing had gained sufficient governmental support by 1975 that the

South Pacific Forum heads of government issued a joint statement affirming opposition to French nuclear testing and support for a regional nuclear-free zone. New Zealand, Fiji, and Papua New Guinea in the same year obtained UN General Assembly endorsement of a South Pacific Nuclear Free Zone. The provisions of the proposed zone, though never adequately clarified, apparently were intended to ban not only nuclear testing within the region but also access by all nuclear-armed or powered ships. The General Assembly resolution was adopted by a vote of 110 to 0 with 20 states abstaining, including all of the nuclear powers except China.

That regional initiative died with the defeat of Labor governments in New Zealand and Australia in 1975. Earlier, however, Australia, Fiji, and New Zealand had successfully challenged French atmospheric testing in the International Court of Justice, and French testing went underground in 1974—but only after some forty-four atmospheric tests. The nuclear-free movement, though still active, progressed no further until new Labor governments in Australia and New Zealand were elected in 1983 and 1984.

By 1983, antinuclear feeling ran high again, particularly in New Zealand. Center and right-wing factions of the Australian Labor party that formed the new Labor government in Canberra believed these and other regional pressures threatened ANZUS and regional security by challenging not only French testing but also U.S. Navy regional access. Canberra argued these pressures could be contained only by early implementation of a nuclear-free zone arrangement that addressed French nuclear testing, as well as the stationing or storing of nuclear weapons and the potential dumping of nuclear waste, but protected essential regional security requirements. The latter were perceived as including freedom of high seas navigation, innocent passage through territorial seas, and port access by "nuclear ships." In short, to preempt more radical proposals, Australia sought establishment of a zone similar to that of the Treaty of Tlatelolco for Latin America.

In contrast with Australia, antinuclear sentiment in New Zealand had become a majority view, though one pressed most actively by the Labor party. That party was elected to office in July 1984 with a commitment to ban access to New Zealand territory, ports, and waters by nuclear-powered ships and nuclear-armed ships and aircraft. The policy's implementation in early 1985 led to the suspension of the U.S.–New Zealand leg of the ANZUS alliance.

The Australian government, meanwhile, had acted on its concerns by proposing its version of a South Pacific Nuclear Free Zone (SPNFZ) at the South Pacific Forum's 1983 meeting. After extended consultations between forum governments and between Australia and the United States, the Treaty of Rarotonga was signed in 1985 and went into effect in December 1986. Australia and several other forum members had taken care to make sure the treaty was consistent with U.S. regional security requirements and public criteria for adherence to nuclear-weapons-free zones. The security requirements are essentially that there be no impediments to regional transits or to regional port and air access.

Publicly acknowledged criteria for U.S. participation in nuclear-free zones are complex, but the essential elements require that the zone arrangement be an initiative of the regional states, acceded to by all nuclear powers; that there be no detrimental disturbance of existing alliance relationships or of maritime and aerial navigation rights and freedom; that it not affect port and air access; that states within the zone be effectively prohibited from developing or acquiring nuclear weapons; and that there be adequate verification arrangements.[3] The SPNFZ treaty and its protocols meet all the above criteria, except for French and British support.

The zone's geographic scope embraces the South Pacific from Australia and Papua New Guinea in the west to the waters off Latin America in the east. It also includes Australian waters and possessions in the Indian Ocean. Given a lack of treaty protocol approval by Great Britain, France, and the United States, geographic gaps are the Pitcairn Islands, French Polynesia, New Caledonia, Wallis and Futuna, and American Samoa.

The Treaty of Rarotonga parallels the Latin America Treaty of Tlatelolco nuclear-weapons-free zone (to which the United States is a party). It bans the testing, stationing, and storage of nuclear weapons within the zone and the acquisition of nuclear weaponry by zone states. It also bans ocean dumping of nuclear waste. The treaty recognizes U.S. freedom of navigation concerns and acknowledges that the issue of port access by nuclear-armed or powered ships remains a decision for each signatory. In short, the treaty did no more than codify existing policies of most of its signatories, including Australia.

The five nuclear powers – Great Britain, China, France, the United States, and the Soviet Union – were each invited to sign and ratify the treaty protocols. The protocols bind signatories to accept zone restraints with respect to their territories within the zone (American Samoa for the United States), abstain from using nuclear weapons against zone states, and refrain from helping others violate zone provisions (that is, assisting French nuclear testing).

The Soviet Union and China signed and ratified the relevant protocols, although Moscow had initially reserved the right to use nuclear weapons against zone states that exercise their treaty right to extend port access to Western nuclear-armed ships. No mention was made of that reservation when the Soviet Union signed the protocols. France refused to accede because such action would require terminating its nuclear testing in French Polynesia. In deference to U.S. and French positions, Great Britain has not signed the protocols.

In 1987 the U.S. government publicly recognized that the zone had been successfully tailored to avoid conflict with essential security requirements in the South Pacific and that the zone satisfied all U.S. public criteria for nuclear-weapons-free zones but one – the one requiring participation by all parties "deemed important" (in this instance, France). U.S. officials also publicly stated that no U.S. actions or policies in the South Pacific were inconsistent with the provisions of the Treaty of Rarotonga and its protocols. Yet the United States decided not to sign the treaty.[4]

That decision was motivated mainly by a concern that acceding would stimulate further nuclear-free movements in other regions (particularly in Southeast Asia), where similar zone arrangements would conflict with security interests requiring the stationing or storage of nuclear weapons. A second important consideration was U.S. support for a French independent nuclear deterrent capability and related acceptance of the requirement to test that capability.

A third factor was a less public element of U.S. criteria—the attainment of nuclear weapons nonproliferation objectives not otherwise feasible. Each of the zone arrangements in which the United States does participate (Latin America, Antarctica, the seabed, and outer space) covers areas where a threat of proliferation existed in the absence of verifiable treaty arrangements. As one major example, several Latin American states possessed the capability and perhaps the will to develop nuclear weapons. The same concern has driven U.S. support for nuclear-weapons-free zones in Africa, the Middle East, and South Asia and thus offsets concern about "spinoff effect." SPNFZ offers no such benefit: all states within the zone had already rejected acquisition of nuclear weaponry (in any event, only Australia has the capability to develop such).

U.S. Defense Department officials have also publicly asserted that the United States should hold open the option to station or store nuclear weapons in American Samoa "to defend U.S. territory."[5] That point is inconsistent with U.S. acceptance of Treaty of Tlatelolco prohibitions on the stationing and storage of nuclear weaponry on other U.S. territory—the Virgin Islands and Puerto Rico. In a related concern, accepting a prohibition of nuclear weaponry in American Samoa could establish an unwanted precedent for U.S. defense responsibility on behalf of a U.S. possession to the Micronesian states in free association with the United States. In contrast to these positions, two U.S. Pacific forces commanders in chief (CINCPACs) – Admiral William Crowe, Jr., and Admiral Ronald Hays – advised then Secretary of Defense Caspar Weinberger that SPNFZ protocol signature and ratification would serve U.S. security interests.[6]

An intangible factor was that the United States considered the issue immediately after New Zealand adopted policy and legislation that in effect banned U.S. Navy port access. A few key senior U.S. officials confused New Zealand's "nuclear-free" position with that of the Australian-promoted SPNFZ treaty intended in part to protect U.S. regional port access.[7]

Some uninformed U.S. officials also asserted that SPNFZ protocol acceptance would close options, such as deployment of nuclear weapons into Australia, that in fact did not exist.[8] Australian national policy, for example, had excluded that option from the early 1970s on and was merely codified by the SPNFZ treaty. Whether the United States is a party to the protocols is irrelevant to the legal position in Australia.

The reaction of Australia and the Pacific islands to the U.S. decision ranged from major disappointment to outrage. They had expected U.S. signature, given the careful tailoring of the Treaty of Rarotonga to satisfy U.S. requirements. One immediate consequence was that the United States lost some credibility with respect to its public positions on arms control measures. A related assumption was that Washington's primary concern was deference to France. The decision not to sign also reinforced a perception among some that the United States viewed the region as a "nuclear playground."[9] The Soviet Union and China's no-cost and risk-free signatures were applauded.

On balance, however, the Australian strategy of defusing pressures among nuclear-free zone protagonists seems to have been successful. Although regional peace groups and leftists have argued that SPNFZ is a sell-out to U.S. interests, there have been no significant pressures for change in the zone's provisions. Pressures against U.S. Navy port access within the region, never serious or widespread, have virtually disappeared. Access currently is denied only by New Zealand, with Vanuatu apparently shifting over to a permissive position. There is continuing quiet regional government pressure on the United States to accede to the SPNFZ protocols, and some pressure from the U.S. Congress.[10] The House of Representatives has twice adopted resolutions urging U.S. signature and ratification of the SPNFZ protocols, most recently in late 1989. The Bush administration, partially in response to these pressures, in early 1989 began a review of the 1987 decision. Subsequent public statements by senior officials have made clear that the review confirmed that decision.[11]

French nuclear testing continued until early 1992 with no signs of change in Paris's position that it is "nonnegotiable." It remains to be seen whether France will resume testing after 1992. France's national position is that it will desist permanently if other nuclear powers do likewise.

The Johnston Atoll Controversy
and Other Environmental Issues

The potential for ocean dumping or other regional disposal of nuclear and other toxic wastes remains a regional concern, but has receded as an issue in recent years. Concern was initially prompted by a 1978 U.S. proposal to use a Pacific island for permanent storage of spent nuclear fuel. Earlier there had been open discussion of ocean dumping of nuclear and other toxic waste, including the possibility of scuttling obsolescent nuclear-powered submarines in deep ocean areas. All of these proposals have been abandoned, and the United States has through various international conventions formally committed itself not to dump nuclear and other toxic wastes in the ocean. The most recent is the Convention for the Protection of the Natural Resources and Environment of the South Pacific Region (SPREP), signed in 1986.

Throughout most of the 1980s, Japan was perceived as the primary environmental threat; it had considered dumping nuclear waste in the Marianas Trench near the Northern Mariana Islands. Pressure from regional states, including formal appeals by the South Pacific Forum, elicited a Japanese commitment not to engage in ocean dumping of toxic wastes.

A new issue was the 1990 U.S. decision to use Johnston Atoll in the North Pacific to destroy chemical weaponry previously based in Germany, as well as that transferred from Okinawa many years earlier. World War II chemical weapons recently located in the Solomon Islands also were earmarked for destruction by the Johnston Atoll Chemical Agent Disposal System (JACADS). Regional and U.S. environmental groups, and many island state governments, have questioned the safeguards involved and the consequent potential impact on the regional environment. The South Pacific Forum, in the communiqué following its 1990 meeting, expressed "grave concern" about the project and about use of the Pacific for disposal of hazardous materials from other regions.

Washington responded to regional concerns with intensive high-level briefings to concerned regional governments, by inviting regional government representatives and the media to visit the site to reassure themselves about safeguards, and by assuring regional governments that the JACADS operation would be terminated after the weaponry described above was destroyed. Following a discussion of the issue at the October 1990 summit meeting of President Bush and regional heads of government, regional leaders seem to have adopted a position of resigned tolerance or acceptance of the project's inevitability and necessity. To some degree, that acceptance has been driven by an emerging awareness that far larger stocks of chemical weaponry (93.4 percent of those held by the United States) were to be destroyed at continental U.S. sites with safeguards similar to those at Johnston Atoll.

Related to the foregoing concerns, several Japanese and

U.S. firms have explored with some island governments (principally Western Samoa, Tonga, the Marshall Islands, Papua New Guinea, and the Solomon Islands) the possibility of using isolated islands for the dumping of nonnuclear industrial waste.

Decolonization

Nine dependent territories remain in the Pacific: those of France (French Polynesia, New Caledonia, and Wallis and Futuna); those of the United States (American Samoa, Guam, the Commonwealth of the Northern Marianas, and, temporarily, Palau); Great Britain's tiny Pitcairn Islands, inhabited by a few dozen descendants of the *Bounty* mutineers; and the Tokelau Islands. The latter by choice remain a New Zealand–administered territory. Among the dependent territories, with a total population of fewer than 400,000, only the futures of New Caledonia and Palau are currently at serious issue. But the outlook for New Caledonia is one of the most problematic, with a potential for twists and turns that could damage some Western and regional state interests.[12] (Palau's future is addressed in chapter 5.)

French and U.S. Pacific territorial policies have many similarities. Both nations assert they have "territories," not "colonies"; both view the territories as integral parts of their nations; both extend citizen or national status to, and generously subsidize, the indigenous inhabitants of their territories; and both attach strategic significance to their territories.

But the similarities end there. Some of the U.S. Pacific territories seek adjustments in their status, but within a framework of a continuing close relationship with the United States. In contrast, the indigenous Kanaks of New Caledonia seek independence from France. In French Polynesia, a growing minority (currently about 15 to 20 percent) favors independence while a current majority favors higher levels of political autonomy. France, unlike the United States in its territories, has actively encouraged metropolitan emigration to New Caledonia to the point that the Kanaks are now a minority. Until recently, France also developed New Caledonia in ways that excluded indigenous participation, a practice with no parallel in the U.S. territories. Finally, the French territories have experienced insurrection, other political violence, and levels of political repression without parallel in the Pacific.

Among the first to colonize the South Pacific, France annexed New Caledonia in 1853, initially for use as a penal colony and naval way station. French settlement followed, with most of the Kanak population confined to reserves and most arable land seized by settlers. Kanak attacks on French settlements were frequent in the late nineteenth century. Insurrectionist activities of the 1980s also had their precedents in the Kanak revolts of 1878 and 1917 in which thousands died.

Following the loss of Algeria and Indochina, France encouraged further emigration to New Caledonia. Polynesians have also immigrated from France's other Pacific territories, as well as Indonesians and Vietnamese. The population at the 1983 census was 43 percent Kanak, 37 percent French, and 20 percent Polynesian, Vietnamese, Indonesian, and others. Today's French community is a mix of descendants of nineteenth-century convicts and settlers (the "Caldoche"), "colons" from Algeria and Indochina, and transient public servants and military.

New Caledonia's monetized economy centers on nickel production, commercial agriculture, and tourism (mainly Australian and Japanese). The poorly educated Kanak community continues to be based on subsistence agriculture with little participation in either the public or private sector. Political rights were granted to Kanaks only in 1951.

Pessimism about any change in their status under French rule led various Kanak political groups favoring independence or autonomy to coalesce in 1984 into the Front de Liberation Nationale Kanak et Socialiste (FLNKS). Loy-

alist party alignments within the French community, supported by other non-Kanak ethnic groups, are primarily
with the right-centrist persuasion in France and include
some educated Kanaks. Many Algerian and Indochinese
colons now living in New Caledonia understandably perceive themselves as being in a "last stand" position.

Although the FLNKS mainstream is essentially conservative and largely nonideological (and has been led by
former Catholic priests), a small extremist group (the Front
Uni de Liberation Kanak, or FULK) developed links with
Libya in 1980 that led to Libyan paramilitary training and
some funding for FULK cadres. The latter remain a fringe
element with little influence on FLNKS policy. FLNKS on
several occasions condemned the FULK association with
Libya and has disavowed FULK policies.

The above polarization resulted in violence in the late
1970s: French settlers assassinated Kanak leaders, and
Kanaks responded. Reciprocal Kanak and loyalist violence
in the 1980s reached levels requiring massive French military and police reinforcements and the first serious French
efforts at political resolution of the territory's political future. Kanak hopes were high with a 1985 offer of "independence in association with France" by the French Socialist
government. But that initiative lapsed with the French conservative election victory of 1985 and a decision by Paris to
suppress the independence movement. Violence escalated;
several Kanak leaders were assassinated by loyalists while
the Kanaks turned to civil disobedience and armed strug-
gle. The latter culminated in the taking of several French
police as hostages in 1988. The bloodletting during and
following French military action to release the hostages
shocked New Caledonia and the Pacific; it seemed to ensure
increased intercommunal violence.

Throughout most of the ten-year period of tension and
increasing violence, a majority of Kanaks boycotted elections and referenda on the grounds that electoral boundaries and rolls were skewed in favor of loyalists. The point
had validity because all French citizens in New Caledonia,

including French civil servants, military personnel, paramilitary police (up to 8,000 during peak periods), and temporary residents were accorded an equal franchise. Transient French elements with little or no vested interest in the territory's future possessed the balance of voting power.

Again, however, French national elections intervened. The Socialists returned to office in Paris in May 1988 with the New Caledonia issue high on their agenda. By August the new Rocard government had managed to achieve an agreement with the FLNKS and key loyalist parties in New Caledonia. The Matignon Accords provide for a major ten-year effort to develop the Kanak community and integrate them thoroughly into the territory's economic and political life. It also calls for a referendum in 1998 offering the choice of independence or continued association with France.

Although the accords have bought time and hope for peaceful resolution of New Caledonia's future, there is concern that extremists, both Kanak and loyalist, may seek to sabotage them. That possibility was evidenced in the May 1989 assassination, by Kanak extremists with Libyan links, of two key moderate FLNKS leaders. Another Kanak concern is the history of broken French political commitments triggered by changes of government in Paris.

For the moment, though, all parties to the accords – France, the FLNKS leadership, and the loyalist leadership – are determined to make them work. The 1989 assassinations of FLNKS leaders also appear to have had a sobering or moderating effect on all parties. Paris and the loyalists now hope that current reform efforts will persuade the Kanaks that their best interests lie in integration into a multiethnic society in continued association with France, but with more territorial autonomy and full Kanak political participation. The Kanaks hope that current reform efforts, including closer cooperation between the Kanak and Caldoche communities, will lead to a multiethnic independent "Kanaky." They pin their 1998 referendum hopes on electoral reform and on changing demographic patterns that together pose the possibility the Kanaks will become a majority of those on the electoral rolls. Some Kanaks also assert, however, that they may not be ready for independence by 1998; between 20 and 30 percent of the Kanak community has opposed independence in the past.

A breakdown of the accords would ensure a return to violence. Given the balance of weaponry and armed forces in New Caledonia, the Kanaks could not mount sustained large-scale guerrilla warfare, but they are capable of levels of civil disobedience and sporadic major violence that would damage the territorial economy and prompt considerable French emigration from New Caledonia. French loyalists in turn have demonstrated a capability and will to respond with equal or greater levels of violence. A regional concern is that failure (or long delays in achieving Kanak political objectives) could radicalize the currently moderate FLNKS and ultimately cause the emergence of an impoverished, unstable, and radical Kanak state. Such a state could threaten the regional interests of Australia, New Zealand, and neighboring island states. A recent RAND Corporation report notes that many Kanak youths have already been radicalized and many are prone to violence.[13]

The outcome of these processes remains uncertain. The two most likely options appear to be an independent "Kanaky" with continuing close relations with France or a form of free association with France similar to that of several Micronesian states with the United States or that of the Cook Islands and Niue with New Zealand. (The latter case provides lower levels of autonomy in internal and foreign affairs and confers New Zealand citizenship on Niueans and Cook Islanders.) Whatever New Caledonia's future status, it probably will provide for division of the territory into autonomous regions based on ethnic content. That process has already begun.

Throughout the Pacific islands, and in Australia and New Zealand, the Kanak cause has received sympathy and varying levels of official support. Particularly in Australia, however, official support was in the recent past tempered by concern for Libyan influence and other potential radical influences and continues to be colored by a desire for a settlement that will ensure a continuing French relationship, including the massive levels of financial subsidy essential to New Caledonia's development and stability. Anglophobic conservative elements in France have been inclined to misinterpret Australian and New Zealand urgings for political change in New Caledonia as representing an effort to displace the French presence and influence with their own.

The South Pacific Forum has consistently supported self-determination leading to New Caledonia's independence, but in a form that would recognize the rights of all ethnic communities. It also has formally welcomed and endorsed the Matignon Accords.

The United States has had no involvement in the issue, but it has endorsed the Matignon Accords and taken the position that New Caledonia's political future should be resolved by peaceful evolution to a status that recognizes the legitimate interests of all communities. Most Kanaks have strong positive images of the United States, a residue of the major U.S. military presence during World War II. A few elites have hostile images flowing from an erroneous perception that the United States supported past French repressive policies. The perception, in turn, flows from public statements by French conservative leaders and Australian and New Zealand leftists. Moderate FLNKS leaders have sought U.S. educational opportunities for Kanaks, U.S. investment in New Caledonia, and dialogue with U.S. officials.

French Polynesia has not yet become a major decolonization issue; a majority of its people continue to favor association with France, although they want higher levels of political autonomy. Unlike New Caledonia's Kanaks, the French Polynesians have not suffered dispossession of most of their land. They also participate fully in the territory's political and economic life and remain the dominant ethnic group. French nuclear testing has brought an infusion of capital resulting in a per capita income higher than any other in the South Pacific, including that of New Zealand.

These data, however, conceal massive distortions in income distribution and major social problems; the latter include high levels of unemployment, particularly among the young. The foregoing problems resulted in riots in 1987 in Papeete, the territory's capital, that left the city looking like a war zone. Current French efforts directed at social reform, coupled with higher levels of political autonomy, may defuse what could otherwise become a volatile situation and regional issue in the 1990s. One probable option is free association.

A related dilemma for French Polynesia is the future of nuclear testing in that territory. Because of the accompanying economic benefits, many (perhaps most) French Polynesians seem to accept the program, albeit reluctantly. Permanent termination of French testing and of related interest in the territory, accompanied by sharp cuts in financial subsidies, could spell economic disaster for French Polynesia.

Tiny Wallis and Futuna is of little significance to France, although that territory totally depends on French subsidies and the emigration of its youth to employment opportunities elsewhere (mainly New Caledonia and French Polynesia). No pressures exist currently for a major change in political status.

Marine Resources

The establishment of 200-mile oceanic exclusive economic zones or EEZs dramatically changed Pacific political and economic geography and the economic prospects of some island states. The zones interconnect and blanket much of the South, Central, and North Pacific. One state, Kiribati, with a land area roughly equal to the greater Washington, D.C., area, exercises jurisdiction over the resources in a zone equal in size to all of Europe. Roughly a third of its government revenues are from licensing fees for fishing fleets operating in its EEZ.

The EEZ seabeds of several states also have major deposits of manganese and other strategic minerals. Seabed mining technology and global supply and demand forces may coincide in the early twenty-first century to provide another significant resource for some of the smaller island states. For the present, however, EEZ tuna is the only major commercial resource of many island states. Licensing fees, after external aid, are the most significant source of government revenues and foreign exchange for several smaller states.

Differing juridical positions on the region's tuna resource placed the United States in direct conflict with island state interests and generated a major crisis in U.S. relations with the region from the late 1970s through 1987. The United States asserted that management and conservation of highly migratory species, in this instance tuna, should be controlled by regional convention. In the U.S. view, no single state deserved jurisdiction over a resource that may be in several different zones over a matter of days or weeks. All other states (except the Bahamas) recognized coastal or island state authority over tuna and other migratory species within an EEZ.

In the absence of a regional fisheries convention, U.S. law and fishing fleets did not recognize the authority of a state to require licenses to fish for tuna within its EEZ. Congress had given teeth to that position in 1976 when it adopted the Fishery Conservation and Management Act (the Magnuson Act) to mandate trade sanctions against, and terminate development assistance for, nations that seize U.S. fishing vessels for violation of jurisdiction claims not recognized by the United States.

U.S. Tuna fleets in the late 1970s began to operate in regional EEZs on a large scale without licensing. From a regional perspective, they were practicing, with U.S. government tolerance, resource piracy. U.S. efforts in the late 1970s and early 1980s to negotiate a regional fisheries convention consistent with the intent of the Magnuson Act failed. The issue came to a head in 1984 when the Solomon Islands seized and confiscated the U.S. tuna clipper *Jean-*

nette Diana. Magnuson Act aid and trade sanctions were imposed, and the United States was portrayed throughout the region as bullying a small island state.

In the wake of the affair, Kiribati and Vanuatu, ignoring Australian, New Zealand, and U.S. expressions of concern, negotiated fisheries agreements with the Soviet Union. Kiribati's president, in response to these concerns, publicly asked why his government should not accept licensing fees from the Soviets when they, like the Americans, could simply pirate that resource.[14]

The combination of regional outrage and the perception of related Soviet inroads finally induced Washington to negotiate seriously and successfully a regional fisheries agreement with the members of the Forum Fisheries Agency. The 1987 South Pacific Fisheries Treaty, though not a regional conservation/management scheme envisaged by the Magnuson Act, nonetheless moots legal differences by being a multilateral arrangement. In return for annual catch zones and quotas, the five-year agreement (which came into full effect in 1988) obligates the United States to provide $12 million annually for five years ($10 million in U.S. economic support fund grants and $2 million from the American Tunaboat Association in licensing fees and technical assistance). The funds are provided to the Forum Fisheries Agency and distributed under formula to affected states. The agreement was applauded in the Pacific. Island state governments and the Forum Fisheries Agency have since pressed Japan to negotiate a similar, comprehensive arrangement (thus far without success) and have sought arrangements with other nations operating fleets in the region.

Further positive developments have included congressional amendment of the Magnuson Act in 1990 to recognize coastal and island state jurisdiction over tuna and other migratory species within their respective EEZs and an associated congressional call for a ten-year renewal of the regional fisheries treaty. The fundamental juridical cause of fisheries issues between the United States and the island states has thus been laid aside, perhaps eliminated. Negotiation of the treaty's extension is in progress. Another U.S. fisheries initiative welcomed by the region was the 1990 decision to sign the 1989 Wellington Convention, which bans driftnet fishing in the South Pacific.

A new concern of the Forum Fisheries Agency and the South Pacific Forum has been Japanese and Taiwanese driftnet fishing practices. The latter amount to marine resource strip-mining; a small fleet in a short time can strip thousands of square miles of nearly all marine life. The Forum Fisheries Agency in 1989 asserted that the practice, if continued, could doom the region's tuna industry within five years. Japan initially was reluctant to halt this practice and at times implied links between levels of development assistance and an island state's position on this issue. The United States supported the South Pacific Forum's call for restraints on driftnet fishing: for example, it cosponsored with New Zealand a UN General Assembly resolution calling for termination of Pacific driftnet fishing by July 1991. The Japanese government in mid-1990 announced suspension of Pacific driftnet fishing. Taiwan's government has also moved to comply with the UN resolution.

4

U.S. Interests and Objectives
in the Pacific Islands

Since the early nineteenth century, the United States has viewed its national interests in the Pacific islands in terms of the islands' geographic relationship to other and more significant regions. The islands were essential stopover points for crew rest and ship replenishment on many of the trading routes linking the Americas with Asia and Australia. Trading vessels were joined by New England whalers and U.S. missionaries in the mid-nineteenth century. Some islands also were important as a source of *guano* – bird droppings that had evolved into organic phosphate, a valued natural fertilizer.

In 1856 Congress adopted the Guano Act, which authorized U.S. ship captains to claim possession of "Guano islands" for the United States. Johnston Atoll in the North Pacific thus became the first U.S. Pacific island possession in 1858. In the years that followed, similar claims were made for Midway, most of the Line and Phoenix islands (now part of Kiribati), most of the islands that today form the nation of Tuvalu, and several of the Cook and Tokelau islands. In nearly all cases in the South Pacific, Britain and New Zealand had conflicting stronger claims and exercised jurisdiction. With decolonization, these claims passed to the Cook Islands, Kiribati, and Tuvalu.

But it was the close of the nineteenth and opening of the twentieth century that brought the United States into the region for fundamental strategic reasons. Annexation of the Philippines, together with perceptions of the future importance of the China trade, in great measure drove the related annexation of Guam and Hawaii. Samoa's relationship at the time to sea-lanes between the Atlantic and the Pacific via Cape Horn, and to the projected Panama Canal, argued for the parallel annexation of American Samoa in the South Pacific. The relationship of these islands to trans-Pacific sea-lanes and the need for coaling stations for the emerging modern U.S. Navy were fundamental considerations in all three acquisitions. Some islands subsequently also became important sites for cable and wireless stations. Wake Island in the North Pacific was annexed in 1899 for that purpose. The development of trans-Pacific commercial aviation in the late 1930s provided a further transportation dimension: the importance of the islands as refueling points for services to Asia and Australia. Nineteenth-century Guano Act claims to some South Pacific islands (for example, Canton) were given new legal status by presidential annexation declarations in the 1930s. Some remained essential to Pacific aviation until the 1960s. Most smaller island claims were, however, relinquished in 1979 and 1980 (see chapter 6). Wake, Midway, Palmyra, Howard, Baker, and Johnston Islands and Kingman Reef are the main residuals in the North Pacific. The United States still claims Jarvis and Swains Islands in the South Pacific.

The 1941–1945 Pacific war added another dimension of interests and national policy objectives. The Japanese thrust through the Pacific islands toward Hawaii in the North Pacific and Australia in the Southwest Pacific prompted a "never-again" policy of "strategic denial": denial of military access to potential adversaries who could threaten U.S. territory and critical air and sea-lanes between the United States and Asia-Pacific friends and allies. That requirement alone led to a major new political presence in the Pacific islands: U.S. administration of the Micronesian islands wrested from Japan in World War II. The Northern Mariana, Caroline, and Marshall Islands in 1947 became the "strategic" Trust Territory of the Pacific Islands. It was the only UN trusteeship so designated and gave the United States carte blanche to deny access to others and use them for defense purposes.

The Pacific islands nonetheless rapidly slipped from the consciousness of most Americans at the conclusion of World War II. The vast array of wartime bases, except those on Guam and in Hawaii, was closed. The only significant defense-related activities elsewhere were nuclear testing between 1946 and 1962 (mainly in the Marshall Islands) and the subsequent development of the Kwajalein Missile Range facility. Another activity was CIA use of Saipan between 1951 and 1962. Chinese Nationalist forces from Taiwan were trained to infiltrate mainland China and conduct guerrilla warfare.

Postwar neglect of the region was perhaps natural. The United States controlled nearly all of the islands of the North Pacific, while all of the islands of the South Pacific (other than American Samoa) were colonies of close allies. Pressures for political change within the region were virtually nonexistent before the 1960s, and nothing threatened vaguely defined U.S. interests. A series of events and trends in the 1960s and 1970s, however, caused Washington to reexamine U.S. regional interests and policies.[15]

In the North Pacific, the UN criticized U.S. neglect of its trusteeship agreement obligations relating to the political, economic, and social development of the Micronesian islands. This criticism prompted the start in 1969 of negotiations to terminate that trusteeship. That development coincided with concern in Washington that Western Pacific political trends threatened U.S. military basing arrangements in the Philippines, Okinawa, and the Japanese home islands. There was a parallel perception of the potential utility of some Micronesian islands, mainly Palau and the Northern Mariana Islands, as fallback options for U.S. forces in the Western Pacific. These quite separate forces together drove the refining of U.S. political and security objectives in the North Pacific.

Parallel to these developments was the South Pacific decolonization process that had begun in 1962 and peaked in the 1970s. Although the process was generally peaceful, the need to define U.S. interests and develop policies relevant to new relationships with the region had become self-evident by the late 1970s. The process continues with global and regional political change, including fundamental shifts in East-West relations and in related threat perceptions.

Security Concerns

U.S. security interests, broader strategic concerns, and related objectives today derive from several fundamental interrelated factors. Above all, the United States is itself a Pacific island nation by virtue of Hawaii, Guam, the Northern Mariana Islands, American Samoa, and special relationships with the Federated States of Micronesia, the Marshall Islands, and Palau. In the South Pacific, the United States has vital interests in Australia, including the ANZUS alliance relationship and the related strategic importance of the South Pacific island nations.

Trans-Pacific air and sea routes remain critical links with Asia-Pacific friends and allies and with the Indian Ocean. The Kwajalein Missile Range facility in the Marshall Islands will remain essential so long as there is a need to test ICBM delivery vehicles and to develop the Strategic Defense Initiative.

A series of related policy objectives flows from these factors. Above all, secure lines of communication need to be maintained throughout the region. That objective in turn requires U.S. naval and air access, denial of adversary military access, and preservation of a friendly and stable political environment.

Although U.S. strategic and security interests in the Pa-

cific islands have been consistent historically, changes in the
character of potential threats and in defense technology have
necessitated change in specific requirements and policy objectives. The development of long-range aircraft and aerial
refueling, nuclear-powered ships, satellite communications,
and intercontinental ballistic missiles together have largely
eliminated what had been so essential in World War II: "step-
ping-stone" island bases throughout the Pacific. These developments do not, however, alter in principle the requirement
of strategic denial, including guarantees that the region's
islands cannot be used for sophisticated intelligence collection (for example, downlinks for satellites).

More than half of the U.S. Navy, and the great majority
of its surface assets, also remains conventionally powered
and requires periodic refueling. All ships require resupply,
crew shore rest, and servicing. U.S. forces would require
access to major regional airports for antisubmarine operations and fleet resupply in any future Pacific war.

The importance of the North Pacific islands in the
above context is obvious. Guam is strategically located and
under U.S. sovereignty. Given its location and small size,
however, as well as the variety of U.S. commitments and
potential contingencies, for the foreseeable future Guam
can be only one element in a broader regional commitment
of U.S. forces, even as some extension of military functions
proceeds in the wake of the abandonment of Philippine-
based facilities. There is neither political nor geographic
scope for significant expansion of Guam's existing major
air and naval facilities. There also are risks associated with
a geographic concentration of a large proportion of regional
military assets.

In the Northern Marianas, immediately north of
Guam, the United States in the 1970s did acquire long-term
leases for much of Tinian Island and for smaller areas of
Saipan for contingency use. Tinian also was seen as suitable
for intermittent Marine Corps exercises. The only use of
either island thus far has been for exercises and, on Saipan,

the recent construction of a radar installation. The latter is part of the broader "Pacific Barrier" network erected to monitor Soviet satellite launchings. At present the Defense Department has no intention of developing major new facilities in these islands even in the face of U.S. loss of access to those in the Philippines.

Palau, the Federated States of Micronesia, and the Marshall Islands, spread across the Pacific between the Philippines and Hawaii, have a limited role with respect to U.S. security requirements. The free association relationship with the latter two of these states, and potentially with Palau, provides the United States with defense responsibility, but also with significant constraints on military use other than routine port and airfield access. Current U.S. requirements and specific arrangements in these islands are as follows.

The United States has no current or projected requirements for military facilities in the Federated States of Micronesia (Yap, Truk, Pohnpei, and Kosrae). The Kwajalein Missile Range facility in the Marshall Islands is secured by long-term political agreements.

In Palau, should the present free association agreement be implemented, the United States would have a narrow range of contingency rights or options:

• U.S. Navy anchorage in Palau's main harbor and a small nearby land area for logistics support
• joint use with civil aviation of Palau's two main airfields and 2,000 acres for logistics support purposes
• periodic access to uninhabited areas for occasional training exercises by U.S. forces, after consultation in each instance with the Palauan government.

By agreement with Palau, the United States will not station or store nuclear, chemical, or biological weapons in those islands.

The "Palau options" are unlikely to be exercised in full

measure, if at all. They were formulated in the early 1970s against a backdrop of a perceived expanding threat to U.S. security interests in the Western Pacific and a related concern about the possibility of losing access to defense facilities not only in the Philippines, but also on Okinawa and in the Japanese home islands. Not only was Palau then seen as a potential site for the relocation of some U.S. military activities, but so were Guam, Saipan, and Tinian. But the small size of these islands, political constraints, cost factors, and the absence of large and skilled labor forces always ensured that few major operations could be duplicated on these islands. The massive ship-servicing facilities at Subic Bay could not be transferred to any of them. For these reasons, but also because of declining threat perceptions, budget constraints, and changing strategic requirements, the Defense Department has no plans to develop new facilities in Palau, even against the background of the loss of access to facilities in the Philippines.[16]

The North Pacific islands do have strategic importance in another sense. Although in peacetime they lie well to the south of many North Pacific sea- and air lanes, a Pacific war—however remote a scenario, especially in light of the close of the cold war with Moscow—would require air and sea movements to shift southward to minimize adversary interdiction. That factor alone drove policies tailored to ensure U.S. access to regional ports and airfields.

The primary U.S. strategic concern in the South Pacific has been and will continue to be security of air and sealanes between the United States and Australia. But another concern stems from the South Pacific being an alternate route to the Indian Ocean. Most peacetime ship movements between the Pacific and Indian oceans are via the Indonesian archipelago straits or the Strait of Malacca. But in the face of an adversary's capability to mine these straits, the United States and its regional allies do not have an adequate mine-clearing capability. Regional states may also attempt to close these straits or interdict shipping. In any of these contingencies, most transits between the two oceans would shift to the South Pacific and to the waters south or north of Australia. The former Soviet Union, long aware of this scenario, conducted extensive hydrographic and oceanographic research necessary for antishipping submarine warfare in the South Pacific.

Some strategists and scientists have asserted that a new security interest relates to the potential development of antisatellite warfare technology, although current congressional restraints severely inhibit testing and prevent deployment. Should this change, the best place to have intercepted Soviet satellites following launch is from a triangular area in the South Pacific northeast of New Zealand and 180 degrees opposite the three Soviet launch sites. As one authority puts it: "Control of areas opposite space launch facilities could deny entry and exit to the respective space programs just as control of Gibraltar or the Strait of Hormuz could deny entry and exit to some critical ports."[17] The capability needed to detect a launch is provided by an existing U.S. space tracking network, including radar installations on Saipan in the Northern Marianas and Kwajalein in the Marshalls.

Aside from the U.S. territories and the Micronesian states in free association with the United States, the United States has no direct security commitments to any of the Pacific islands. The 1979 Treaties of Friendship with Kiribati and Tuvalu require consultations in the event of a threat to either state and require that neither provide military access to third parties without prior consultation with the United States. The primary purpose of these treaties was formalization of U.S. relinquishment of claims, dating back to the nineteenth century, to several Kiribati and Tuvalu islands. The consultative clauses were essential to satisfy conservative U.S. senators who otherwise would have attempted to block ratification of the treaties.

Most island states and what were the three active ANZUS partners nonetheless accepted that ANZUS provided an informal security umbrella over the South Pacific in that a threat to or an attack on any state in the region could pose a threat to Australia, New Zealand, or the United States. Communiqués issued after annual ANZUS ministerial meetings frequently stressed that the partners have a direct interest in the territorial integrity, peaceful development, and stability of the region's states. With the demise of ANZUS ministerial meetings in 1985, subsequent bilateral Australian-U.S. ministerial meetings occasionally have been followed by similar affirmations.

ANZUS treaty commitments can be triggered not only by an attack on the chief metropolis of the partners, but also by an attack or threat of an attack on their forces and territories in the Pacific area. As a hypothetical example, U.S. security obligations would arise if Australian forces were attacked when responding to an island state contingency.

Despite the absence of formal security relationships in the South Pacific, there has been modest U.S. defense cooperation (exercises, training, military equipment transfers, and security assistance grants) with Papua New Guinea, Fiji, and Tonga, although cooperation with Fiji was suspended following the 1987 military coups. Much of the defense cooperation with Fiji related to Fiji's major contributions to Middle East peacekeeping forces. U.S. forces for some years also have participated extensively in regional disaster relief and public works ("civic action") construction projects.

The requirements of U.S. security interests in the Pacific islands clearly are modest. For the most part they relate to future contingencies rather than present need, and they are satisfied by existing arrangements. U.S. relationships with its territories and with the Micronesian states ensure strategic denial of adversaries in the North Pacific and essential U.S. access.

No U.S. bases are sought or are required in the South Pacific. Denial of adversary military access seems certain for the future. With the exception of New Zealand, U.S. forces currently have reasonable access everywhere.

Political Objectives

To a greater degree than security interests, U.S. political interests and objectives in the region derive from a combination of regional and global considerations. They can be summarized as follows:

- regional acceptance of the United States as a supportive global and regional power and of its Pacific territories as regional partners in their own right
- full regional and international acceptance of the Micronesian states as sovereign entities responsible for their own foreign affairs (now achieved)
- termination of the UN trusteeship agreement's application to Palau through early implementation of free association arrangements acceptable to a majority of Palauans
- preservation of stable, friendly, and democratic governments that can serve the developmental and other aspirations of their peoples and that pursue foreign policies consonant with fundamental U.S. and other Western interests
- preservation of the region's generally excellent human rights record
- encouragement and support of regional cooperation organizations essential to the region's development and stability
- peaceful conclusion of the decolonization cycle in the French territories of the South Pacific and continuing regional acceptance of the relationships American Samoa, Guam, and the Northern Marianas have with the United States
- regional acceptance of the special partnership roles of Australia and New Zealand
- encouragement of Japan's emerging major role in regional economic development
- encouragement of the developmental roles being taken by other major Western allies (particularly Great Britain, Germany, and France), as well as those of the EC and major international institutions such as the Asian Devel-

opment Bank, the World Bank, and the UN Development Program

- exclusion or at least limitation of hostile external influence and activity.

The foregoing political interests and objectives are generally self-evident, parallel those of many other regions, and are discussed elsewhere in the context of challenges, opportunities, and policy responses.

Economic Interests

Of the three sets of U.S. interests—security, political, and economic—the latter are the least significant. The United States in 1987 exported only $340 million in goods to the Pacific islands and imported goods valued at only $349 million. U.S. investment in the region is small, and the potential for expansion is limited, with the exception of Papua New Guinea where U.S. companies have invested about $1 billion in the development of gold, oil, and natural gas resources. The potential for seabed mineral resource development is a major regional asset that may attract U.S. capital in the future. The region is the globe's primary source of tuna, with the U.S. catch currently running at about $300 million annually. Other, limited trade and investment opportunities within the region are generally not pursued by the U.S. private sector because of lack of awareness, though they may increase through official encouragement.

U.S. economic interests thus can be defined as access to regional marine resources and markets and continuation of the favorable investment climate. As a function of broader U.S. interests in Japan, Australia, and New Zealand, their continued economic access also is important to the United States. Within the region, it is important that there be enough economic and social development to sustain political stability.

It is readily apparent that U.S. interests and objectives

in the Pacific islands are modest relative to those in most other regions. Few of the objectives are vital, except those that relate to broader security interests in Australia, East Asia, and the Western Pacific and to global East-West competition. U.S. regional interests and objectives also parallel the regional interests of Western friends and allies, particularly Australia, New Zealand, and Japan. Of major importance to U.S. relationships with the Pacific islands, most U.S. interests and objectives are compatible with those of regional states and in many instances actively serve them.

Oceania clearly has been a low-threat environment since World War II. Basic U.S. regional interests have suffered few significant external challenges, and the region generally was not subjected to much superpower competition and confrontation found in most other Third World regions. With the end of the cold war and the receding potential for East-West conflict, external threats to U.S. interests in the Pacific islands are now at an even lower level.

5

U.S. Policy in the North Pacific

Spain colonized the Mariana (including Guam) and Caroline Islands in stages between the sixteenth and nineteenth centuries, primarily because of their relationship to sailing routes between Spanish colonies in the Americas and the Philippines. Germany colonized the Marshall Islands in 1885.

With the transfer of the Philippines to the United States following the 1898 Spanish-American War, Spain's Pacific colonies were no longer relevant to Spanish interests. All were put up for sale, but Washington purchased only Guam. Germany bought the remainder. The short-lived German presence ended early in World War I when Japan seized the Northern Marianas, Carolines, and Marshalls without firing a shot.[18] Following the war, they were placed under Japanese administration as a League of Nations Mandate. Unlike its predecessors and the United States, Japan thoroughly colonized, developed, and fortified the islands. All were integrated into the Japanese economy.

Koror [in Palau] became a stylish oriental metropolis with a population of 30,000, streetcars, and factories that manufactured beer and fireworks. Koror had public baths, laundries, dressmakers, tailors, masseurs,

barber shops, butcher shops and rug stores. There were
41 ice dealers, 77 geisha girls, one fortune teller, a zoo
and 55 restaurants, 13 of them considered upper-class.
Palauans had never seen anything like it before, and
they haven't since, either.[19]

World War II placed Micronesia on the front pages of the
U.S. press for the first time as U.S. forces campaigned
through the islands in Pacific battles. Saipan and Peleliu
were among the bloodiest, while Tinian became a major base
for B-29 missions against the Japanese home islands, including the flights that devastated Hiroshima and Nagasaki.

The trauma of the Pacific islands campaigns and related
decisions late in the war to maintain forward deployment of
U.S. forces in the Western Pacific ensured a "never-again"
U.S. political strategy for Micronesia. U.S. official views of
the latter's future, as the war in the Pacific entered its last
months, were naively but bluntly expressed by then Secretary of War Henry L. Stimson in January 1945. He said
that annexation of Micronesia

by the United States does not represent an attempt at
colonization or exploitation. Instead it is merely the
acquisition by the United States of the necessary bases
for the defense of the security of the Pacific for the
future world. To serve such a purpose they must belong
to the United States with absolute power to rule and
fortify them. They are not colonies; they are outposts,
and their acquisition is appropriate under the general
doctrine of self-defense by the power that guarantees
the safety of that part of the world.[20]

But outright annexation was not politically feasible.
The United States had already promoted the principle that
the prewar League of Nations mandated territories should
become trust territories administered by UN members with
an obligation to develop them toward self-government or
independence.

The pragmatic decision thus was to place Micronesia

within the trusteeship system, but in a manner that would ensure nearly absolute U.S. political control. While all other trusteeships were placed under the jurisdiction of the UN General Assembly, Micronesia was designated a "strategic" trust territory under the authority of the UN Security Council, with the trusteeship agreement between the council and the United States. The latter's veto authority in the Security Council guaranteed no future change in Micronesia's status without U.S. consent. In the Security Council's 1947 debate of the trusteeship agreement, Ambassador Warren Austin's justification for this arrangement differed little from that of Secretary Stimson in 1945.

> Tens of thousands of American lives, vast expenditures of treasure, and years of bitter fighting were necessary to drive the Japanese aggressors back from these islands. These islands constitute an integrated strategic physical complex vital to the security of the United States. The American people are firmly resolved that this area shall never again be used as a spring-board for aggression against the United States or any other member of the United Nations.[21]

The agreement was concluded in 1947, and Micronesia, as the new Trust Territory of the Pacific Islands, remained under the administration of the U.S. Navy until 1951. It, together with Guam and American Samoa, were then transferred to the Department of the Interior.

Micronesian Crosscurrents: The Trust Territory of the Pacific Islands

The United States had acquired a complex area for whose management it had little relevant experience. Micronesia's islands are scattered over an area of the North Pacific equal to the U.S. mainland's, but have a total land area of only 700 square miles (about half the size of Rhode Island). Fewer than 100 of the islands are inhabited. The population of about 75,000, although for the most part Micronesian, includes culturally different groups speaking nine separate languages and having little in common with each other except a history of foreign domination. The islands' only resource of any importance to the United States was land: a scarce asset of critical political, economic, and social importance to the Micronesians and, in some areas, of potential strategic value to the United States.

The first fifteen years of U.S. administration of Micronesia were characterized by what has been charitably described as benign neglect. Some U.S. government reports in the 1960s observed that the per capita income of Micronesians in the early part of that decade was only a third of what it had been under the Japanese. Towns, road networks, port facilities, and other infrastructure not already destroyed by the war decayed and were overcome by jungle. The U.S. appropriation to administrate and develop the territory was limited to $7 million annually between 1947 and 1962, and even that amount was seldom expended. Access to most of the territory was limited to U.S. officials and those with special permits until the early 1960s. The exclusion policy was driven partially by security concerns related to nuclear testing in the Marshall Islands and a CIA-operated Nationalist Chinese guerrilla training base on Saipan.[22] But an equal factor was the influence of anthropologists who had convinced the U.S. Navy and the Interior Department that the Micronesians and their cultures should be protected from external influences. Many observers described that policy as the "zoo theory of administration"; some also called the trust territory the "rust territory."

In the early and mid-1960s Australian and British-led UN visiting missions severely and accurately criticized the United States for the absence of economic development, the inadequacy of social services, and the lack of progress toward self-government or independence. Independent studies commissioned by the U.S. government in the same period offered the same criticism. Although President Kennedy in 1962 had determined that "U.S. policy is the movement of Micronesia into a permanent relationship with the United States within our political framework," a major U.S. study mission in 1963 found that U.S. neglect was so complete that the United States risked losing political control.[23] The resulting Solomon Report recommended that priority be given to the territory's political, economic, and social development and that programs be introduced that would generate political sentiment in favor of U.S. territorial status.[24]

The criticism, however, brought little immediate reaction; President Kennedy's assassination occurred only days after the report was completed. The new Johnson administration was preoccupied with other priorities. But UN and other criticism continued and forced the beginnings of change in the mid-1960s. A territorywide legislature, the Congress of Micronesia, was established in 1965; it became a major force for political change. Annual budget support and other grants were increased nearly tenfold in the space of a few years. Priority was given to education, health and other social services, and infrastructure development.

An unintended but fundamental force for political change was establishment of a massive Peace Corps presence in 1966 – with some 700 volunteers in peak years. The volunteers brought with them the frustrations of U.S. youth directed at Washington, the Vietnam War, and associated U.S. policies. The impact on the political directions of Micronesia was enormous; the volunteers reinforced Micronesian distrust of Washington and concern for Washington's defense planning for Micronesia. Compounding this effect, most of Micronesia's emerging political elites were exposed to the antiestablishment and anti-Vietnam War sentiment present at U.S. universities in the mid- and late 1960s.

A somewhat hyperbolic comment in 1968 by Amata Kabua, who eventually rose to be president of the Republic of the Marshall Islands and then president of the Micronesian Senate, is representative of the attitudes of Micronesian elites toward the U.S. administration in the late 1960s and early 1970s:

With only a few exceptions, Micronesia has been subject to a succession of unskilled, unqualified, inept, dis-
interested administration personnel . . . many of them,
according to the Americans themselves, rejects from
other government posts. They have patronized us to an
offensive degree; they have promised us everything for
the use of our islands; and they have given us nearly
nothing. Our roads, according to American visitors, are
the worst in the world. Our hospitals exist only in dis-
trict centers, and are in most cases a disgrace. The
public educational system is so bad as to be tragic.
Economic help is nil, resources development non-exist-
ent. . . . Unfortunately, it has come to the point where
it is difficult for the Micronesian to believe anything
the U.S. administration says—everything smacks of
the idle promises we have been listening to for the past
20 years. The result of this is that the Micronesian no
longer takes the U.S. administration seriously.[25]

But there also was recognition of U.S. contributions to
democratization. A 1969 report of the Future Political Status Commission of the Congress of Micronesia commented:
"Whatever our particular evaluations of the U.S. administration may be, we feel that one contribution has been indel-
ible, one achievement almost unqualified: the idea of democratic, representative, constitutional government. . . . "[26]

Pressures for change within Micronesia, particularly
among educated young political elites, emerged amid growing Washington concern about the prospects of U.S. military access to facilities in the Philippines, Okinawa, and the
Japanese home islands. Leading U.S foreign affairs and defense journals of that period were replete with articles pro-
jecting the loss of nearly all military facilities in the Western Pacific and predicting the consequent requirement of
maintaining forward deployment of U.S. Pacific forces in
Micronesia.

The foregoing prompted acceleration of political and social development programs. If the value of program services
are included, the annual U.S. subsidy to Micronesia in-

creased to nearly $300 million by the mid-1980s – about
$2,500 per capita. In misguided but well-intentioned zeal,
many U.S. domestic social services, such as the food stamp
program, were extended to Micronesia in the 1970s. The net
effect was to destroy much of the traditional subsistence
economy. U.S. educational programs also were introduced
but often had little relevance to the Micronesian environment. Little effort was made to develop limited economic
resources or to attract private investment capital.

The paucity of the trust territory's resources coupled
with modernization processes made aid-dependence inevitable and probably permanent. But the excesses of U.S. generosity in the late 1960s and the 1970s led to Micronesian
economies today that consist almost entirely of a massive
public service sector and a small private sector servicing
the needs of the former. Aid-dependency levels are among
the highest in the Pacific, as are urban unemployment levels (more than 80 percent in some areas).

Responsibility for this state of affairs can be attributed
to Micronesia's leadership as well as to the United States.
Although it was the latter that offered a broad range of
social services and other programs ill suited to the Micronesian environment, Micronesian public servants and legisla-
tors usually made the ultimate decisions to accept these
programs. The roots of the problem were well-intentioned
but ill-informed Interior Department officials and U.S. con-
gressmen who initiated the extending of these programs to
Micronesia.

U.S. political objectives throughout the 1960s and early
1970s remained unchanged and were assumed to be consistent with the wishes of the Micronesian people: termination
of the UN trusteeship and annexation of the Micronesian
islands as a U.S. territory. Washington believed that the
fundamental requirements of strategic denial and forward
deployment could be protected by only that political course.
That this objective was not consistent with the obligation
to develop Micronesia toward self-government or independence was little understood or simply ignored. It was

assumed in any event that the Micronesians would vote overwhelmingly for a territorial relationship in an act of self-determination. There also were the related problems of bureaucratic inertia, turf consciousness, and other inter-agency conflicts. The attitudes of Defense Department offi-cials had changed little from those of War Secretary Stim-son in 1945. The Interior Department resisted any change that would significantly erode its authority. It also as-sumed that congressional interior committees would op-pose any political status for Micronesia other than that of a U.S. territory. The Department of State argued for imple-mentation of trusteeship agreement obligations but was overridden by the Defense and Interior departments in in-teragency decision making. At the senior policy-making level, lack of concern was characterized by a remark attrib-uted to then National Security Adviser Henry Kissinger: "There are only 90,000 people out there. Who gives a damn?"[27]

Acting on these flawed assumptions and attitudes, the Interior Department and representatives of the Congress of Micronesia in 1969 opened negotiations on the future politi-cal status of the trust territory.

Termination of the Trusteeship

U.S. objectives encountered disaster in two negotiating ses-sions in 1969 and 1970. The Micronesians firmly rejected any form of territorial status. They instead sought the sta-tus of sovereign states in free association with the United States and the unilateral right to terminate that relation-ship in favor of full independence. The only alternative to free association, they asserted, was independence. Microne-sian objectives were for the most part based on the Cook Islands' free association relationship with New Zealand.

Washington's inadequate understanding of political change in Micronesia reflected a fundamental historical problem. After annexing the Philippines, Guam, American

Samoa, and other foreign territories at the turn of the century, Washington never acknowledged that it had become a colonial power. And in the absence of that recognition, Washington never established a professional colonial service or a consistent territorial policy with clear objectives. The total focus on the strategic character of U.S. relations with Guam, American Samoa, and the Trust Territory of the Pacific Islands was typified by their administration by the U.S. Navy until 1951. In that year, all were transferred to the jurisdiction of the Department of the Interior.[28] But the Interior Department and its congressional oversight committees often appeared unable to discern differences between Indian reservations and distant territories. In the case of Micronesia, part of the problem was the absence of any systematic means of reporting and analyzing developments, political and otherwise, as a basis for Washington to formulate viable policies.

The trust territory's administration was staffed by political appointees and other officials having little or no relevant experience. Compounding that problem, many officials had little or no knowledge of any existing policy. They usually operated on the basis of their own instincts and preferences and sometimes at cross-purposes with existing policy. Few, if any, had ever read the trusteeship agreement. During the author's service in Micronesia in the early 1970s, one senior U.S. official based on Saipan vigorously and publicly advocated union of Micronesia, Guam, and American Samoa into a single "state." It was never clear whether he wanted an independent state or U.S. statehood! Various U.S. programs also conflicted with U.S. policy. One example was the introduction into Micronesia in the late 1960s and early 1970s of Peace Corps lawyers and then Office of Economic Opportunity lawyers who frequently advocated Micronesian independence. These legal programs were a credit to the openness of the U.S. system and to U.S. efforts to fulfill trusteeship obligations – but they also conflicted with policies directed at a territorial relationship.

The failure of the first effort at negotiating Micronesia's future led the White House, under pressure from the departments of Defense and State, to reassess the Department of the Interior's management of the future political status process. An immediate consequence was the author's assignment in late 1970 to trust territory headquarters on Saipan. He was tasked with establishing contact with Micronesia's political leadership, with setting up a reporting and analysis system to advise Washington on developments (political and other) relevant to formulation of policy, and with acting as liaison between Micronesia's leadership and those in Washington responsible for negotiating the future status of Micronesia.

Responsibility for the negotiations and the development of related policy and strategy in Washington was transferred from the Interior Department to a presidential personal representative for Micronesian status negotiations. This representative was supported by an interagency office recruited primarily from the Defense and State departments.

The foregoing actions were paralleled by reassessment of U.S. objectives and related policy. But another negotiating effort in 1971 also failed, mainly because Washington did not understand or accept the pressures for political change that had emerged in Micronesia. An offer of commonwealth status (a modified form of territorial status), intended to take into account Micronesians' concerns for the protection of their land from Department of Defense eminent domain authority seizures, was flatly rejected, except by the Northern Marianas. Essential elements of the problem were Micronesian distrust of the United States and exaggerated perceptions of U.S. defense planning for Micronesia. The latter arose from the open debate in Washington of Micronesia's potential role in the forward deployment of forces following a fallback from bases elsewhere in the Western Pacific.

Washington regrouped and in 1972 agreed to negotiate a free association relationship, a process that continued into the 1980s and remains to be finalized. Initially, the United States had also hoped to negotiate an arrangement that would embrace all of the Micronesian islands. Because of regional cultural and political differences, however, that objective was not viable. The only thing the geographically, culturally, and linguistically different elements of Micronesia had in common was the U.S. administration and a determination to achieve political change. Later separate negotiations with the Northern Marianas between 1972 and 1975 led to the establishment of the Commonwealth of the Northern Mariana Islands in 1986. That status was approved by an overwhelming majority in a 1975 UN-observed act of self-determination. The inhabitants of the Northern Marianas are now U.S. citizens with U.S. sovereignty over their islands. They have a high level of internal self-government, but the United States retains defense and foreign affairs responsibilities.[29] Generous financial terms provided about $228 million in federal grants and services between 1986 and 1992. In 1988 alone, the Northern Marianas received $52.5 million in grants and services, or $2,610 per capita. (The only other U.S. jurisdiction to be subsidized at a similarly high level is Washington, D.C.: $2,604 per capita in 1988.)[30]

Negotiations with the remaining Micronesian islands for a single free association relationship also failed. Subsequently, in 1986 the Republic of the Marshall Islands and the Federated States of Micronesia (the Caroline Islands less Palau) emerged in separate free association relationships with the United States. UN-observed acts of self-determination took place in each case. For complex reasons addressed below, a third free association agreement with Palau remains to be implemented, and the UN trusteeship agreement still applies to that island group.

The negotiation process was more protracted than necessary, and the outcome probably more expensive for the United States than had to be the case. U.S. negotiating strategy was flawed for most of the seventeen-year process by several elements. Above all, there was a tendency in the earlier years to exaggerate the potential utility of Micronesia for U.S. forward deployment in the Pacific and the political arrangements essential to protect U.S. interests. That in turn enhanced Micronesian expectations, demands, and leverage in the economic negotiations.

U.S. negotiators until the late 1970s also asserted that independence was not a political option available to Micronesia. That position created two related problems (aside from its conflict with trusteeship agreement obligations). It reinforced sentiment in Micronesia for independence (although never to the point that it became a majority position) and provided the Micronesians with a political lever to obtain concessions to offset the absence of an independence option. The United States ultimately accepted independence as a political option mandated by the UN trusteeship agreement. By the time that concession was made, the free association package was virtually complete.

Most other major concessions made by U.S. delegations were similarly offered too late to achieve the desired effect: early conclusion of an agreement. By the time such concessions were made, often after a delay of years, the Micronesians in frustration had moved to other positions requiring further time-consuming negotiation and other concessions.

Many people involved in the negotiations today agree that relatively modest U.S. concessions between 1970 and 1972 could have led to early agreement on closer and less costly political relations than those that have emerged. Most would also agree, however, that U.S. relations with these islands are best served by the highest possible level of Micronesian self-government. Some also believe that the ultimate arrangements – the compacts of free association – are so complex and riddled with built-in potential conflicts that U.S. and Micronesian interests would have been better served by Micronesian independence and a simpler treaty relationship. It is argued the latter would be more acceptable to the international community and would provide a sounder base for the fundamental requirement of U.S. interests in Micronesia: an amicable rather than an adversarial relationship. Others assert that the precision of the compacts minimizes the potential for conflict arising from differing interpretations. Almost all agree that one fundamental fact currently bonds the Micronesian states and the United States: each needs the other, and neither currently has practical alternative options.

The Micronesian states in free association with the United States today are sovereign and fully responsible for their internal and foreign affairs. They have the right to terminate the relationship in favor of full independence. Their levels of autonomy are in fact significantly greater than those of the original model: the Cook Islands' free association relationship with New Zealand. New Zealand has far higher levels of residual or reserve authority, and Cook Islanders continue to be New Zealand citizens. The citizens of the new Micronesian states do, however, have unfettered access to the United States, including opportunities for employment. The products of the two states for the most part also enter the United States on a free trade basis.

The United States is obligated to defend these states and their people "from attacks or threats thereof as the United States and its citizens are defended."[31] The compacts also provide that the Micronesian states will refrain from actions inconsistent with U.S. defense responsibilities and that the United States can exclude any form of third-party military access.[32] Compact defense provisions run for fifteen years from 1986, even if the free association relationship is terminated.

The United States also is committed to provide the Marshall Islands, the Federated States, and Palau approximately $3.3 billion in grants over fifteen years, plus a broad range of U.S. federal programs and services. (The commitment to Palau will be fulfilled only with implementation of that free association relationship.)[33]

The Future of Palau

U.S. defense rights in the free association relationships have a complex history that has frustrated implementation of that status in Palau. The Micronesians early in the political status negotiations insisted that all present and potential U.S. defense requirements in their islands be precisely defined and agreed to before implementation of the new relationships. U.S. Defense Department assessment in 1971 of current and projected military requirements in the region ultimately led to agreements for the continuation of the Kwajalein Missile Range facility in the Marshall Islands, naval and air access everywhere, and the "Palau options" described in chapter 4.

Palau's free association compact differs from the others in that the financial and defense provisions will run for fifty years from implementation, even if Palau should terminate free association in favor of independence. (The longer term was suggested by the Palauan negotiating delegation.) A further difference is that the U.S. defense obligation to Palau is more akin to that of a mutual security treaty than the obligation in the other compacts. The other compacts mandate defense of the Federated States and the Marshalls as if they were U.S. territory. The Palau compact provides only that the United States, in the event of an attack or the threat thereof, "would take action to meet the danger to the United States and Palau in accordance with its constitutional processes."[34] The weaker defense commitment flows from another compact provision that states that the United States shall not "use, test, store, or dispose of nuclear, toxic chemical, gas or biological weapons" in Palau.[35] (A similar provision in the compacts with the other two states bans such weaponry only in peacetime.)

Complicating the foregoing, Palau has adopted a "nuclear-free" constitution that, together with Palau Supreme Court interpretations, also bans any temporary or transit presence of nuclear weapons and all forms of nuclear power. These provisions conflict directly with U.S. defense responsibilities in a free association relationship. Given the U.S. policy of neither confirming nor denying the presence of nuclear weapons on U.S. ships and aircraft, neither vessel would have access to Palau. This U.S. policy has not been formally abandoned, despite President Bush's September

1991 announcement that the United States would remove all of its seaborne tactical nuclear weapons. Under Palau's constitution, U.S. nuclear-powered ships would not have access even in the absence of the weaponry issue.

The constitution does provide that its nuclear-free provision can be overcome by a 75 percent majority in favor of free association in an act of self-determination. Seven UN-observed acts of self-determination over seven years (the last on February 6, 1990) provided majorities ranging from 60 to 72 percent in favor of free association, not enough to satisfy that requirement. An alternative remedy offered in another clause of Palau's constitution provides that the constitution can be amended by a simple majority in three-fourths of Palau's sixteen states in a constitutional referendum. The Palau government is considering that possibility with a view to reducing the constitutional requirement for approval of free association to a simple majority. If that course is successful, an eighth act of self-determination would require only a simple majority to implement the free association relationship. There is, however, considerable opposition in Palau to amending the constitution.

Palau since 1981 has been (by virtue of U.S. restraint with respect to the exercise of authority provided by the UN trusteeship agreement) self-governing, except for foreign affairs and defense. The evolution of that self-government has been plagued by chronic and occasionally violent political instability (including the assassination of Palau's first president and the suicide of his elected successor), corruption, and fiscal policies that have brought Palau to the edge of bankruptcy.[36] The problems had become so severe by 1989 that some elements of U.S. administration of Palau were being reintroduced in 1990: primarily Interior Department veto authority over Palauan legislation. This reversal of self-government was a consequence of U.S. congressional pressures arising from a 1989 report on Palau by the U.S. General Accounting Office.[37]

Palau's progress toward termination of the trusteeship also has over time been complicated by Soviet and peace group disinformation that significantly damaged the U.S. image in the Pacific. The standard disinformation line emphasized that the United States promoted economic dependence, political violence (including assassination), and corruption to coerce an unwilling nuclear-free Palau into free association. It was also alleged that the United States would then build a Trident submarine base and store nuclear, chemical, and biological weapons in that remote and small group of islands.

This line of reasoning has ignored fundamental facts, above all that the free association agreement prohibits the stationing or storage of nuclear or toxic weaponry in Palau and that the United States does not base Trident submarines outside of the United States. If the United States wished to engage in these actions, it would seek continuation of the trusteeship, which places no such restraints on U.S. defense activity.[38] The allegations also have ignored the fact that UN teams have observed all Palauan acts of self-determination. These teams have certified that the acts that produced large majorities in favor of free association were fairly and appropriately conducted.

Few outside Palau also understand that the nuclear issue is in some degree superficial and covers an underlying cultural problem: traditional Palauan regional and clan rivalries. The resulting rivalry between those in office (who favor free association) and those out of office, who use the nuclear issue as a convenient political tool to solicit international sympathy and support, has led to massive interference in Palauan politics by non-Palauan peace groups.[39] An unfortunate side effect has been the emergence within Palau of exaggerated notions of its importance to the United States and a resulting tendency to attempt to extort higher subsidies from the United States.

The only legitimate nuclear issue is whether U.S. ships (including those that are nuclear-powered) and aircraft will be able to visit Palau without confirming or denying the presence of nuclear weapons (i.e., on the same basis as visits to all other states that accept U.S. ship and aircraft visits).

That issue is resolved in favor of the U.S. position by the compact of free association with Palau.

Palau's course remains uncertain pending possible revision of Palau's constitution to permit an act of self-determination that would require a simple majority to approve free association or changes in the free association relationship that could generate a 75 percent majority vote. Other political options are equally difficult. Independence and a treaty relationship with the United States are a theoretical possibility but probably would not be supported by a majority of Palauans. Many (perhaps a majority) of those who oppose free association in fact favor a commonwealth or other closer relationship, not independence. But a closer relationship with U.S. sovereignty would require scrapping Palau's present constitution, an act that would be politically difficult if not impossible. If free association is to be pursued and continues to require a 75 percent majority, the United States may have to limit its defense options further to minimize that issue.

Another potential problem is that Washington's perceptions of Palau's strategic importance have declined sharply since the compact negotiations concluded. That factor, coupled with growing U.S. budgetary restraints, could easily mean that any effort to alter the compact would reduce the financial benefits for Palau. The compact's present provisions, including the financial commitment, are embedded in existing U.S. legislation.

Free Association Today

As Palau's future political status continues to be an issue, the other Micronesian states have, with U.S. encouragement, entered into the region's political life. They are now full members of the South Pacific Forum and other key regional organizations. They also have established diplomatic relations with a number of states (principally in the

Asia-Pacific region) and have opened embassies in Washington, D.C., and other capitals. The United States in turn has embassies in the capitals of the two Micronesian states.

Although relationships between the Micronesian states and the United States are evolving well, problems may lie ahead. The states' uniquely high levels of dependence and the associated perception of restraints on freedom of political action may, with the next generation of Micronesian leaders (as it has with the second generation of political leaders in the South Pacific), generate frustration and a compulsion to experiment with new links. Compounding that problem might be conflict associated with the network of U.S. federal services and programs operating in Micronesia.

Domestic decisions on U.S. programs and services can be made in Washington with little or no awareness of their impact on Micronesia. Both Micronesian and U.S. interests could be well served by seizing opportunities to simplify the relationship – for example, by replacing U.S. federal programs and services with Micronesian counterparts.

The international community has accepted the new status of the Micronesian states more slowly than desirable because of the way the United States terminated the trusteeship agreement with the UN Security Council. Although there are no precise precedents, most lawyers and others familiar with the UN system agree that the appropriate form of termination would have been UN Security Council endorsement of that act. But it was clear in 1986 that the Soviet Union would veto termination and insist that independence was the only appropriate political status for Micronesia. There also was no precedent for piecemeal termination of a trusteeship with continuing, if temporary, application to Palau.

Faced with the certainty of a Soviet veto, the United States in 1986 had no choice but to terminate the agreement (except for Palau) unilaterally by informing the Security Council that it had fulfilled its obligations and was implementing the new political relationships. To have done otherwise would have been a failure to respond to the wishes of those most directly concerned – the Micronesian people. But even some of the United States's closest friends and allies could not accept the U.S. action. As prime examples, the British, French, and other European governments did not accept unilateral termination and refused to recognize the political entities that have emerged. That lack of recognition created serious practical problems for the new Micronesian states. At one level, their passports were not recognized, making it difficult to travel in Europe and elsewhere for Micronesian citizens. At another level, Micronesian state membership in key international organizations was rejected, as was the states' accession to important international treaties.

The end of the cold war and rapidly improving Soviet-U.S. relations did bring about, with U.S. encouragement, a major shift in the Soviet position in late 1990. At year's end, Washington and Moscow agreed on the text of a UN Security Council resolution that recognized termination of the trusteeship (except for Palau) and acknowledged the new status of the Federated States, the Marshall Islands, and the Northern Mariana Islands. The Security Council on December 22, 1990, approved the resolution by a vote of fourteen to one; only Cuba cast a negative vote. (See chapter 8 for further discussion of the evolution of the Soviet position on this issue.)

The council's action ends the international recognition problems cited above. The two freely associated states are likely to quickly expand the range of their bilateral and international organization relations.

Ironically, more than twenty years after the Micronesian political status negotiations started, one of the fundamental U.S. strategic requirements then driving policy toward Micronesia – forward deployment of forces in those islands as a consequence of a fallback from elsewhere in the Western Pacific – has never materialized. No new bases or other military facilities have been built anywhere in Micronesia (except one small radar installation on Saipan), and

no major new installations are likely to be established anywhere in these islands.

The Northern Mariana Islands,
Guam, and American Samoa

The Northern Marianas commonwealth relationship, implemented in 1986, is likely to last, but is experiencing major
growing pains. Pressures are emerging in these islands for
changes in the relationship that are not consistent with
U.S. sovereignty and citizenship. As some observers put it,
the Northern Mariana Islands seek the benefits of a close
U.S. relationship, plus those of free association or independence. In December 1990, in an effort to keep political status options open, the commonwealth government tried un-
successfully to block UN Security Council termination of
the trusteeship agreement. The commonwealth government
also now asserts that sovereignty was never vested in the
United States and that the United States thus has no authority over the exclusive economic zone of these islands.
Another issue has been an effort to solicit and receive aid
from other nations on a government-to-government basis.
Washington has rejected these and other initiatives by the
Northern Marianas.

These developments have not gone unnoticed in Guam—
particularly the Northern Marianas' relationship with the
United States, which is more autonomous than Guam's.
Guam now also seeks a commonwealth relationship with the
United States. That development unfortunately is paralleled
by emerging indigenous Chamorro nationalism and pressures to give priority status to Chamorros (over against other U.S. citizens on Guam). There is additional pressure, as in
the Northern Marianas, for a level of autonomy inconsistent
with U.S. sovereignty and citizenship.

Distant and conservative American Samoa is also
starting to press for higher levels of self-government. Although proud of their U.S. linkage, those on American Sa-

moa understand how the change in U.S. relationships with North Pacific islands and other precedents can serve Samoan interests within the framework of a continuing permanent relationship with the United States. American Samoa almost inevitably will pursue commonwealth status or perhaps a form of free association that would allow for U.S. national or citizen status.

In all three areas – the Northern Marianas, Guam, and American Samoa – there is frustration with what inhabitants view to be a mix of paternalism, incompetence, and insensitivity in the Office of Territorial Affairs of the Department of the Interior, the agency that oversees territorial affairs. That factor alone generates much of the current pressure for political change in all three U.S. Pacific possessions.[40]

American Samoa and Guam remain "non-self-governing" dependent territories by UN definition and thus, with the remaining French territories, are among the last significant vestiges of Western colonialism. Thus far, the South Pacific community has not applied regional political pressure for the United States to change its territorial relationships, in part because the territories clearly wish to retain a political relationship with the United States. Also, the regional focus has been on the French territories, where there have been major, even violent pressures for political change. The French in recent years have demonstrated a new sensitivity to their territorial problems and, as discussed elsewhere, are responding with policies designed to resolve them. They have already granted higher levels of autonomy than exist in the U.S. territories. When and if the issue of the political future of the French territories is resolved in ways acceptable to those territories and the region, the United States could in turn be exposed to regional decolonization pressures. That is likely, however, only if the United States has not adequately responded to pressures for change in its own territories. Although territorial leaders have not yet appealed for regional political support for their initiatives, they may in the near future if present levels of frustration are not reduced.

6

U.S. Policy in the South Pacific

The United States possessed one major political asset as decolonization began in the South Pacific: an enormous reservoir of good will dating back to the nineteenth century reinforced by World War II. That good will was paralleled by images of U.S. generosity and leadership.

These images carried with them expectations reinforced by strong cultural traditions regarding the role of leaders. Most simplistically put, island leaders are expected to be responsible for the welfare of their followers. This responsibility includes sharing material wealth. Expectations of traditional leaders have been transferred to some degree to relationships between the new states and external powers. The United States asserts that it is a global and regional leader and is accepted as such in the South Pacific. But with that leadership goes responsibility toward the region, a responsibility that most South Pacific elites believe the United States has inadequately fulfilled. The expectations remain, but resentment grows over absence of fulfillment either of the expectations or of some specific commitments.

Formulating a South Pacific Policy

No clearly defined U.S. policy existed for the South Pacific until the late 1970s; Washington had perceived the region as a backwater requiring little attention and as the primary responsibility of Australia, Great Britain, France, and New Zealand. Throughout most of the 1960s and into the mid-1970s, the United States was preoccupied with Vietnam and then with Watergate. By 1977, however, developments in the region could no longer be ignored. The decolonization cycle had peaked; there were the early Soviet regional initiatives, emerging pressures for a regional nuclear-free zone, and pressure from Australia and New Zealand to play a more active role within the region.

These developments led in 1977-1978 to the first major review of U.S. regional interests and to the first comprehensive regional policy statement.[41] The latter emphasized the limited role envisaged for the United States relative to that of Australia and New Zealand.

> Our own interest in the region is inescapable. It is part of the Pacific community to which we are tied by geography and history as well as by growing economic interest. A stable, economically healthy South Pacific contributes not only to the peace and well-being of American territories in the region, but also to the broader interests of the United States.
>
> We do not need to develop massive programs for the South Pacific; this would be contrary to the interests of the islands and our own. Nor should we seek a dominant role as initiator, helper, and guide. We do not wish in any way to impinge upon the sovereignty of these free peoples or to usurp the leadership role that belongs to them and to their near neighbors, Australia and New Zealand.
>
> To sum up, we see the orderly development of the South Pacific region as a contribution to the stability

of the broader Pacific community. Our joint efforts there are still another way in which we strengthen our historic ties with our ANZUS allies and work together for our mutual interests.[42]

The United States also committed itself to expanding its regional diplomatic presence and engaging in higher levels of dialogue; establishing a regional development assistance program and expanding U.S. Information Agency cultural and educational exchange programs; strengthening cooperation with regional organizations, especially the South Pacific Commission, which includes replacing politically appointed U.S. representatives with experienced diplomats based in the region; and designating a deputy assistant secretary of state to be responsible exclusively for Australia, New Zealand, and the Pacific islands. The Peace Corps' regional presence, originally established in 1966, also was expanded. Numbers have fluctuated over the years, but there are now some 400 volunteers in twelve Pacific islands states and territories, including the Federated States of Micronesia and Palau.

Washington also relinquished antiquated and doubtful claims to numerous islands belonging to the new nations of Kiribati, Tuvalu, and the Cook Islands and to New Zealand's Tokelau Islands dependency. This was accomplished through the 1979 treaties of friendship with' the first two island states, a similar treaty with the Cook Islands in 1980, and a fourth with New Zealand on behalf of Tokelau in the same year. As indicated in chapter 4, U.S. Senate ratification of the first two treaties required defense consultative clauses. The United States retained jurisdiction over several small and uninhabited islands (e.g., Howland, Baker, and Jarvis) next to Kiribati. Kiribati is likely to seek transfer to itself of these islands. Except for the limited value of the marine resources in their surrounding exclusive economic zones, they are of no importance to the United States.

Regional Perceptions of U.S. Policy

Island state governments greeted the announced U.S. policies and programs with enthusiasm, with the exception of an assumed surrogate role for Australia and New Zealand. But, as time passed, the perception emerged that the policy offered more rhetoric than substance. Most regional leaders believe the United States failed to or inadequately fulfilled most of the commitments in the following ten years.[43]

Except for appointing a resident ambassador to Fiji (previously there had been a chargé d'affaires with the ambassador living in New Zealand), and very small staff increases in the two regional embassies (Port Moresby and Suva), the U.S. diplomatic presence did not change. Until recently, dialogue also remained at fairly low levels. Only one island state head of government (Fiji's prime minister in 1984) had been invited to visit Washington.

Regional governments were disappointed in 1984 when the Department of State abolished the position of deputy assistant secretary for Australia, New Zealand, and Pacific islands affairs. These relationships were placed under a deputy responsible primarily for relations with China, Mongolia, and Hong Kong.

A regional development assistance program was established, but it was funded until 1988 at minuscule levels: $3 million to $7 million annually, or less than 2 percent of total annual, all-source development assistance to the South Pacific. South Pacific governments argued that the levels reflected U.S. lack of interest in and insensitivity to regional requirements and inadequately reflected either U.S. regional interests or the level of support given to those interests by regional states.

Regional political leaders also argued that a 1977 decision to channel U.S. development assistance to regional and private voluntary organization projects (rather than funding projects on a bilateral government-to-government basis) was politically flawed. Awareness in the region of U.S. contributions to regional development was near zero, as was the political impact of those contributions. Island state governments also complained that the above method of distributing aid showed insensitivity to island state sovereignty. (A small bilateral program was established in Fiji in the mid-1980s, primarily in approving response to reversal of Fijian policies banning nuclear-armed and -powered ships from Fijian ports and waters.)

In defense of primary reliance on multilaterally distributed aid, many island governments are ill equipped to deal with the legal and administrative complexity of formal bilateral assistance programs. Establishing many such programs also could mean that a high proportion of development assistance is absorbed by administrative costs. The regional approach was seen as cost effective, and most projects did in fact foster the development of individual island states.

The United States did become more active in the South Pacific Commission: there was, for example, expanded support of commission projects and strengthened cooperation with other organizations. These positive actions were offset, however, by significant shortfalls in recent years in payment of dues to the South Pacific Commission.[44] In further failure to adhere to policy commitments, the United States reverted in the early 1980s to the practice of politically appointing U.S. representatives to the South Pacific Commission. The appointees generally have lacked any relevant experience or skills and too often have had little interest in the commission. On issues critical to all island states, therefore, the United States was perceived as being insensitive to the region's concerns.

For much of the past twenty years, no regional issue has elicited a more heightened emotional response than French nuclear testing in the South Pacific, and no regional initiative has had broader support than the South Pacific Nuclear Free Zone. These issues are discussed in detail in chapter 3. It suffices to say here that the U.S. failure to sign and ratify the protocols of the zone treaty, after the latter had been tailored to satisfy U.S. regional security requirements and criteria for adherence to nuclear-weapons-free zones, damaged the U.S. image and credibility considerably in the region. Perhaps even more damaging was the long-standing conflict over jurisdiction of tuna resources in island state EEZs and U.S. "piracy" of that resource. Although the issue was satisfactorily resolved in 1987 (see chapter 3), some of the public relations damage lingers. That imbroglio also undoubtedly contributed to the first Soviet regional policy successes (see chapter 8).

The idea that Australia and New Zealand serve as surrogates for the United States is a misinterpretation of a legitimate U.S. view—that is, given shared interests and objectives in the region, coupled with Australia's and New Zealand's own special roles and interests there, the United States looks to them to play a lead Western role. The surrogate image unfortunately has prevailed and is resented throughout the region. Ironically, a major reason the island states want more active U.S. regional involvement is to offset or balance a pervasive Australian and New Zealand presence.

Underlying the foregoing problem is the broader concept of burden sharing. The United States has consistently argued that the allies must equitably share the costs of deterring conflict and the related requirements of promoting political stability and excluding hostile influences. Because the United States contributes the major share of military deterrence in the Pacific, it asserted the idea, now less applicable since the end of the cold war, that Australia and New Zealand should carry the major burden for regional security and development in the South Pacific, a region of primary strategic significance to them. More recently, the burden-sharing concept has been extended to Japan, at least with respect to contributions to regional development. There is some concern, however, about Tokyo's ability to formulate effective aid programs in the islands. These concerns flow from regional perceptions of Japan's insensitivity toward or at least unfamiliarity with regional concerns and its propensity to link aid to commercial interests.

As fair as burden sharing may be, it has hidden costs. Island state governments, like those of other recipient states, are likely to be most receptive to the specific needs of other nations that have supported their own needs. Regional leaders argue that the United States has taken more than it has given and that it has not reciprocated their support in the United Nations and elsewhere or their acceptance of U.S. regional security requirements. The traditional U.S. argument that it contributes to regional security through costly Pacific force deployments has seldom been much appreciated by an emerging generation of island leaders and other elites who perceive no external threats.

In sum, burden sharing is arguably a valid and (given U.S. resource restraints) essential regional political strategy, but it should not be carried to the point of delegating nearly all regional responsibility to friends and allies. More simply put, effective pursuit of some U.S. interests and their requirements will always mean having to apply some U.S. resources.

Yet another problem is the widespread perception that U.S. relations with the region are governed primarily by security interests and concerns, as was evidenced by a U.S. diplomatic tendency to be driven by reaction to Soviet initiatives. In the absence of Washington perceptions of specific Soviet or other challenges or threats to U.S. interests, the region has generally been underattended. Until recently, this perception was fairly accurate, given the correlation between perceived Soviet challenges and various U.S. regional policy initiatives. In another instance of Washington's past neglect of the region, the Department of State failed in regularly training and adequately making use of regional specialists.

Finally, forces beyond U.S. control have damaged the U.S. image. In small island societies concerned about the influence of external forces pervaded by widespread antinuclear feeling, U.S., Australian, and New Zealand leftists and peace groups have been highly successful in promoting widespread acceptance of the allegation that the United

States has attempted to blackmail an unwilling and nuclear-free Palau into free association with the United States to place nuclear bases in those islands. That the allegations make no sense, given any objective evaluation of the Palauan scene and the nature of free association, is irrelevant. As always in politics, perceptions count, not facts.

Another example of damaging allegations is the widespread acceptance of the idea that the CIA encouraged and supported the 1987 coups in Fiji, purportedly because the deposed elected government was about to adopt policies, similar to those of New Zealand, that would ban the U.S. Navy from Fiji's ports. The charges were nonsense, as shown by the U.S. condemnation of the coups, suspension of bilateral development assistance and defense cooperation, and a cutting back of diplomatic dialogue with Fiji. These are hardly the actions to be taken against a government put in place by the CIA.

A further image problem is the reasonably accurate perception that the United States has supported French nuclear testing in French Polynesia, and a false perception that the United States endorsed past French policies in a New Caledonia regionally viewed as repressive and inconsistent with self-determination. The failure of the United States to counter these kinds of allegations effectively illustrates the inadequacy of its public diplomacy in the islands.

Offsetting some of these negative images, Honolulu-based CINCPACs (Commanders in Chief, U.S. Pacific Forces) in recent years have demonstrated their awareness of the connection between political and security interests and of the need to cultivate island governments and elites. Their activities have been multifaceted and generally well received. They have supplied generous disaster relief, sent military civic action teams to assist in public works projects, made personal visits to many island states, provided high-level hospitality in Honolulu for visiting island leaders, and developed defense cooperation programs beneficial to key regional states and to the United States.

A 1990 initiative of Congressman Stephen J. Solarz

may in fact hand to the Defense Department and CINCPAC the single largest U.S. goodwill project in the postwar South Pacific. A defense appropriations measure passed in late 1990 provides $5 million in military construction monies for a new parliament house in the Solomon Islands. The project is linked to the 1992 commemoration of the fiftieth anniversary of the battle for Guadalcanal Island.[45]

U.S. South Pacific Policy Today

The basic tenets of U.S. South Pacific policy as enunciated in 1978 remain sound and have been implicitly reaffirmed on many occasions by U.S. officials in 1990.[46] By 1987, however, U.S. relations with the South Pacific as well as its image there were at their lowest point ever as a result of inattention, broken or flawed implementation of policy commitments, the SPNFZ decision, and the fisheries imbroglio. Recognition of the situation, together with concern about Soviet regional inroads, led to reassessments of U.S. policy implementation and programs and to related new initiatives.

The two existing embassies (Fiji and Papua New Guinea) were strengthened with staff and budget increases, and small new embassies were opened in 1988 in the Solomon Islands and Western Samoa. Dialogue with governments throughout the region was significantly increased, with more frequent visits to regional capitals by senior Washington-based officials. A further welcome development was the reestablishment in 1989 of a deputy assistant secretary of state position for Australia, New Zealand, and Pacific islands affairs. Of particular importance, Washington accepted the South Pacific Forum invitation in 1989 to participate in a postforum meeting dialogue. U.S. Information Agency programs also were strengthened in the late 1980s but were cut back again in 1989 and 1990 because of new budget constraints.

The region has been disappointed by recent reaffirmations of the 1987 decision not to adhere to the SPNFZ treaty protocols. Regional governments, on the other hand, have been grateful for effective U.S. support of their efforts in the United Nations and elsewhere to end driftnet fishing by Japan and others in the Pacific. They also see the 1987 U.S. regional fisheries treaty as a model for fisheries relationships with other nations, particularly Japan.

U.S. development assistance increased in fiscal year 1988 to $22 million, with $100 million then projected for the five years ending in FY 1994 (see table 5). Half that amount, however, was to be in $10 million annual grants to the Forum Fisheries Agency as payment for regional tuna fishing rights. Regional governments perceive that amount as a fisheries fee, not aid. Recent aid budget cuts and emerging other priorities now make it problematic that the $100 million five-year program will be fully implemented. Development assistance dropped to $18.3 million in FY 1989 and was about $16.5 million in FY 1990. The latter sum is lower than 1987 levels if fisheries treaty monies are excluded from the total. U.S. South Pacific aid has thus remained minuscule relative to that given by Australia, Japan, New Zealand, Great Britain, France, and the European Community. It also contrasts unfavorably with the assistance provided to the two small Micronesian states of the North Pacific in free association with the United States: $154.6 million in 1988.

There are no plans to establish multiple formal bilateral aid programs, but recognition of resentment of the regional approach has led to a new strategy of identifying most projects on an informal bilateral basis and implementing them through private contractors. Priority is being given to economically focused initiatives, mainly in marine resources and agriculture but also in health services. Although this shift in methodology has been welcomed by island governments, many continue to press for formalized bilateral programs and for the channeling of U.S. development assistance through governments rather than private contractors. The use of contractors apparently is viewed as a continuing

TABLE 5
U.S. Development Assistance, Grants, and Services,
Fiscal Year 1988 (U.S. $ thousands)

	ODA^a	ESF^b	Totals
1. South Pacific States: Development Assistance (ODA) and Fisheries Agreement Economic Support Fund (ESF) Grants			
Cook Islands	$ 553.0	$ 196.3	$ 749.3
Fiji	$3,381.0^c$	296.3^c	$3,644.3^c$
Kiribati	1,081.2	1,596.3	2,677.5
Niue	508.9	193.3	705.2
Papua New Guinea	3,975.4	3,096.3	7,071.7
Solomon Islands	943.8	596.3	1,540.1
Tonga	1,232.9	26.3	1,259.2
Tuvalu	749.0	596.3	1,345.6
Vanuatu	1,046.3	196.3	1,242.6
Western Samoa	1,484.5	296.3	1,780.8
Subtotal	$14,956.0	$7,060.3	$22,016.3
2. Free Association States: Grants and Services			
Federated States of Micronesia			103,400.0
Republic of the Marshall Islands			48,300.0
Fisheries Agreement ESF Grants			$2,907.0^b$
Subtotal			$154,607.0
3. U.S. Territories: Grants and Services			
American Samoa			48,100.0
Commonwealth of Northern Mariana Islands			52,200.0
Guam			106,300.0
Palau (trust territory)			27,400.0
Subtotal			$234,000.0
Total (categories 1, 2, and 3)			$410,623.3

[a]ODA for each country includes prorated value of benefits of regional projects.
[b]$10 million in ESF grants are obligated under the South Pacific Fisheries Treaty with member states of the Forum Fisheries Agency. Data shown for each country are based on the prorated share of the regional tuna catch. [Editor's note: Because of the author's death, we were unable to verify why the figures in this column, do not add to the total.]
[c]Bilateral development assistance to Fiji was in suspension in FY 1988 because of the 1987 military coups. Data shown include benefits from regional programs, disaster relief, fisheries treaty ESF entitlements, and Section 416 wheat sales as an offset to a reduction in Fiji's U.S. sugar quota.

Sources: As cited for table 3, p. 36.

slight to state sovereignty. There also is a perception that formalized bilateral programs can lead to higher levels of U.S. aid.[47]

Another weakness in administering aid is lack of flexibility. Virtually all development assistance is earmarked for relatively large projects; there is no capability to fund small projects on short notice, even though these projects often are the most visible and politically effective. One remedy would be to establish ambassadorial discretionary funds at a level of $50,000 to $100,000 annually, which each embassy could disburse on its own initiative. Australia's and New Zealand's diplomatic missions in the South Pacific have such funds and use them to good effect.

Of marked importance, President George Bush's propensity for high-level personal diplomacy has been extended to the Pacific islands. For the first time, island state heads of government visiting the United States have found ready access to the president. This was evident with the launch of six such White House meetings in 1989 and 1990, compared with one for all previous U.S. administrations. Bush also held the first summit meeting with Pacific island heads of government—at the East-West Center in Honolulu on October 27, 1990.[48]

The island leaders, as anticipated, brought up the issues of low levels of U.S. development assistance to South Pacific states, French nuclear testing, the U.S. failure to accede to the SPNFZ treaty protocols, and other perceived environmental threats (principally global warming and U.S. plans to destroy chemical weaponry on Johnston Atoll). The president offered little hope for significant changes of U.S. positions in any of these areas. He reaffirmed the view that global strategic considerations precluded SPNFZ adherence and commented that the United States has no influence over French nuclear testing. He also reaffirmed the U.S. view that insufficient data exist to justify major new environmental measures directed at global warming. He balanced that assertion by citing a major new research effort to be funded at about $1 billion annually; he promised to share the resulting data and analysis with regional governments. As indicated in chapter 3, he also obtained resigned acceptance of the Johnston Atoll project by providing personal assurances that the facility will be closed down after its current program is completed.[49]

President Bush brought to the summit his own agenda of new U.S. regional initiatives. Although most represented a repackaging or extension of existing programs, taken together they have potential importance. The most important are the following:[50]

• He proposed establishment of a high-level "Joint U.S.-Pacific Islands Commercial Commission" that would meet regularly to promote private sector trade and investment. There would be a major focus on export trade, tourism, infrastructure development, fisheries, the environment, and human resource development—with enhanced technical assistance and training in some of these areas. Major new efforts would be undertaken to promote U.S. private sector awareness of regional trade and investment opportunities. Annual commission meetings would coincide with those of the South Pacific Forum. U.S. representatives would be senior officers from the departments of Commerce and State and other U.S. agencies.

• The quasi-governmental Overseas Private Investment Corporation (OPIC) was to organize and lead a group of U.S. investors to the region in 1991 to explore investment opportunities. The existing OPIC Asia-Pacific Growth Fund, which has a targeted capitalization of $200 million and is now focused on Southeast Asia, would begin making investments in the Pacific islands. Funding of this project would be private but managed and insured by OPIC. OPIC's global Environmental Investment Fund was to be extended to the Pacific islands with a focus on sustainable agriculture, forest management, ecotourism, renewable and alternative energy sources, and pollution prevention and abatement technologies. The fund has a targeted initial capitalization of $100 million in private sector funds; OPIC insures its projects.

• Aid projects in marine resource development and management, market access, environmental protection, and commercial agriculture were announced that would total about $25 million over several years. Although most of these projects were already in place or in the planning stage, and little new funding is involved, their packaging as a presidential initiative may protect them from future budget cuts.

• A major new educational initiative was proposed, essentially extending to the Pacific islands the Asia-Pacific Economic Cooperation Partnership for Education (announced by Secretary of State James Baker in Singapore in July 1990). The program, drawing on governmental and private sector resources, was to establish new links between U.S. and regional educational institutions and new private sector internships for islanders studying in the United States. There also was to be some expansion of existing training programs for islanders in the United States and within the region.

• Three small new U.S. Information Agency educational exchange programs were announced: (1) Two prominent U.S. private sector leaders were to visit the region annually to assist in fostering the role of private sector economic development. (2) Two presidential fellowships were to be offered annually to island state cabinet-level officials for a program of research, consultation, and lecturing within the United States. (3) Two groups of six senior island state officials were to be invited each year to visit the United States for consultation tours that will focus on different themes. Suggested topics include tourism, forest development and preservation, mineral resource development, environmental issues, and small business development.

The president also confirmed that the United States would seek to negotiate extending the popular South Pacific Regional Fisheries Treaty, request Senate ratification of the Convention for the Protection of the Natural Resources and Environment of the South Pacific Region (SPREP), and sign the Wellington Convention. The latter bans driftnet fishing in the South Pacific (see chapter 3 for discussion of these measures).

At the end of the day, the act of dialogue itself was undoubtedly the single most important contribution to shoring up U.S. relations with the Pacific islands. Although somewhat disappointed by the unchanging U.S. position on key issues to island leaders, the leaders gave President Bush generous praise. Cook Islands Prime Minister Geoffrey Henry, in concluding public remarks, welcomed the president's initiatives. He also stressed:

> We in the Pacific have tended to think that your country is too far away, too concerned with the problems of other places, and you weren't interested in the problems of the people of our region. You have changed that quite considerably, single-handedly. . . . You have, by this single act, begun to replenish the pool of goodwill that has begun to dry up since the last war, the goodwill between the Pacific islands and the United States of America. Don't allow it to dry up.[51]

Another positive development has been major improvement in U.S. relations with nonaligned Vanuatu. Before 1988 there was little contact of any kind. Since Vanuatu's most ardent advocate of nonalignment and of ties with Libya, the Soviet Union, Cuba, and Vietnam was dismissed from the government, Vanuatu's foreign policy shifted markedly toward closer relations with the United States. That change is evident in the small Peace Corps program and security training project now established in Vanuatu, as well as in Vanuatu's request for the opening of a U.S. embassy in Port Vila, the capital.

As a consequence of the 1987 Fiji coups, the U.S. relationship with that key state remains delicate. A new ambassador arrived in Fiji in 1988 after a long gap. For humanitarian reasons and as a response to first efforts to restore a constitutional government, bilateral aid was theoretically restored in 1989. U.S. budget constraints have, however, inhibited implementation of that decision. Defense cooperation probably will remain suspended until Fiji makes a significant move toward restoring democracy (the 1992 election may be an augury on this score). An unrelated problem troubling the relationship is that the United States is in arrears $152.7 million in assessments for UN peacekeeping operations. Fiji, as a consequence, is "out of pocket" $21.5 million for the costs of its contribution of forces to UN Middle East peacekeeping operations (about 6 percent of Fiji's budget). Resentment is compounded by the fact that Fiji participated in these operations largely because of U.S. encouragement. Other problems in U.S. relations with Fiji flow from the imposition of quotas on the importation of Fijian textiles and from occasional differences over the levels of Fiji sugar imported against U.S. sugar import quotas.

In hindsight, U.S. South Pacific policy has been through four cycles since regional decolonization began in 1962. From that date through 1976, U.S. policy awareness could be characterized at best as totally inattentive. The newly inaugurated Carter administration in 1977 reacted to accelerating change within the region, Soviet initiatives, and allied pressures with the first comprehensive South Pacific policy. That new attentiveness and sensitivity to regional issues evaporated in 1981 at the beginning of the Reagan administration. Carter administration policy commitments were shelved or reversed, and a new cycle of inattention continued until 1987. Washington then refocused on the region, but only after the U.S. image had been heavily damaged through neglect and the fisheries imbroglio. Recognition of that, and concern over new Soviet initiatives, spurred new attention and new initiatives. Good policy and intentions have, however, been undercut by new budget constraints.

The Bush administration in turn focused even higher levels of Washington attention on the South Pacific. South

Pacific reactions to many recent U.S. initiatives have been positive, although the initiatives generally are perceived as being only steps in the right direction. It is too early to gauge the ultimate impact of President Bush's summit proposals. Their success will depend largely on the responsiveness of U.S. private sector capital at a time when the U.S. economy is troubled. The fact also remains that regional investment opportunities are limited and are almost nonexistent in some of the smaller states. Most that exist are of such a small scale that they have traditionally not attracted U.S. capital. Besides the risk that summit-generated expectations will not be adequately satisfied, there is the problem that the Honolulu initiatives do not respond to the needs of the smaller and most aid-dependent states.

Fundamental regional concerns about some major aspects of U.S. policy remain, especially with respect to levels of U.S. development assistance in the South Pacific, the global warming issue, and the SPNFZ treaty. Given current budget constraints and emerging new demands on U.S. aid elsewhere, the outlook for major increases in South Pacific development assistance is bleak. There is little hope for U.S. accedence to the SPNFZ treaty protocols in the near future. There also appears to be little likelihood that the U.S. position on responses to the global-warming threat will soon change on a substantial, cost-bearing scale. As other industrial nations implement measures to reduce carbon dioxide emissions, U.S. emissions may expand proportionately, bringing increased resentment in Oceania and elsewhere.

One fundamental positive fact does remain: the problem for the United States in the South Pacific is not a rejection of U.S. involvement; it is a concern for the adequacy of that involvement. Opportunities thus do exist to replenish the regional reservoir of goodwill.

7

Australia, New Zealand, and Other External Powers

Australia and New Zealand, of all Western states, have the most direct strategic interest in the Pacific islands; they are part of the region. Links to the islands date to the origins of the two nations, but particularly to the early twentieth century when both became regional colonial powers in their own right: Australia in Papua New Guinea and Nauru, and New Zealand in Western Samoa, the Cook islands, Niue, and the Tokelau Islands. Although these islands were decolonized in the 1960s and 1970s (with the exception of Tokelau, which is still a New Zealand territory), Australia and New Zealand remain the dominant external influence in each as well as in the former British colonies. New Zealand also perceives itself as having a special affinity with the Pacific islands by virtue of proximity, its own small size, and a large Polynesian population of island immigrants and indigenous Maoris.

Both have economic interests in the region, primarily in service industries (for example, banking, insurance, trading houses, transportation). Australia also has a major investment in the mineral resources of Papua New Guinea. The primary importance of the islands to Australia and New Zealand, however, always has been strategic. The islands of the South Pacific sit astride key sea- and air lanes of communication to the north of both nations, but especially the lanes linking them to the United States and Japan. The islands in turn dominate the northern approaches to both nations, particularly Papua New Guinea vis-à-vis Australia. The Japanese thrust southward into Papua New Guinea during World War II permanently established that point in Australian strategic analysis.

On the global stage, Australia is a major middle power while New Zealand is a minor actor with little influence. They are, however, the superpowers of the South Pacific. Both maintain diplomatic missions in nearly every island state, are members of every significant regional organization (including the South Pacific Forum—of which they are the only non-island state members), and are major sources of official development assistance. Australia is the region's largest source of development aid—$296.8 million in 1988.

Both countries also provide significant security assistance and defense cooperation to the island states in the way of training, grants, equipment, intelligence, and joint exercises. Australia has provided patrol boats to many island states, and the Australian and New Zealand air forces provide aerial surveillance of island state exclusive economic zones. With the exception of New Zealand's defense responsibilities for the Cook Islands and Niue (both in free association with New Zealand), neither has explicit defense commitment agreements with island states that, in the event of an external threat, mandate more than consultations. There is little doubt that Canberra or Wellington would respond to external threats or attacks. Their own national interests would require such action. This particularly applies to Australia's defense relationship with and interests in Papua New Guinea.

Although Australia and New Zealand are quick to assert that they are not surrogates for the United States, their shared regional interests ensure that their influence is generally directed at objectives also serving U.S. and broader Western interests. For instance, they sought to deny the Soviet Union regional military access or political influence.

They promote economic and social development and encourage the related political stability that serves common strategic and related interests.

With one possible if unlikely exception, neither Australia nor New Zealand perceives any significant possibility of an external attack on any of the island states other than those that might be incidental to an unlikely regional or global conflict. There is, however, an uneasiness in Canberra about the potential for problems along Papua New Guinea's common land border with Indonesia should a bellicose and adventuristic Sukarno-style nationalism reemerge in Jakarta. Consequent conflict between Indonesian and Australian forces would also have implications for the United States; article 5 of the ANZUS Treaty confirms that the security commitment applies to an armed attack on the forces of the partners anywhere in the Pacific. Joint Chiefs of Staff Chairman Adm. William Crowe, Jr., and Secretary of Defense Richard Cheney, in public statements in 1988 and 1989, each recognized the applicability of ANZUS in the unlikely event of conflict between Australian and Indonesian forces.[52] Gratefully, relations between Indonesia and Papua New Guinea have recently improved substantially, and the prospect of a serious falling out is slim.

Of greater immediate concern to both Canberra and Wellington is the political instability of several states, particularly Papua New Guinea, Fiji, and Vanuatu. Given Australia's special relationship with and interests in Papua New Guinea, Canberra is especially concerned about the potential for fragmentation of that island state. Australia and New Zealand also share a broader concern that island frustrations with aid dependency and related traditional political links could lead to actions inconsistent with Australian, New Zealand, and other Western interests. Ironically, the problem arises in part because of Australia and New Zealand's regional interests and generosity. There is some regional resentment of their pervasive presence and influence. Their influence has ebbed sharply in Fiji as a result of frequent public criticism from Canberra and Wellington of

Suva's failure to restore a full measure of democracy after the 1987 coups.

A major Australian and New Zealand concern is New Caledonia's political direction should current efforts fail to resolve its future peacefully. Some Australians have described the troubled territory as their future Cuba. Related to all of the foregoing is concern about regional involvement by external mischief makers, especially considering past Libyan activities in Vanuatu and New Caledonia.

Australia and New Zealand also accept the possibility of a Pacific Grenada or other contingency requiring armed intervention, if only to provide support to a friendly government under domestic siege or to evacuate their nationals. They are tailoring forces for such possibilities. Canberra's current concern is the Bougainville secessionist rebellion in Papua New Guinea. Australia thus far has limited itself to logistics support for Papua New Guinea's forces, but military intervention under extreme circumstances, especially to evacuate nationals, has not been ruled out.

Australia attaches the highest importance to its ANZUS alliance with the United States and to an effective U.S. military presence in the Pacific. Canberra thus shares U.S. concern that regional antinuclear sentiment has the potential to limit U.S. military access. Although Canberra was a prime mover in the development of the South Pacific Nuclear Free Zone, it successfully promoted tailoring of the zone treaty to make it compatible with U.S. regional security requirements. The Australian government perceived its moderate proposals as a sensible compromise essential to ease pressure for more radical arrangements that would have banned regional access by nuclear-armed and -powered ships.

In contrast to the Australian government's position and that of the majority of Australians, a small but vocal, well-organized, and sometimes influential fringe of Australian and New Zealand political life is at the forefront in mobilizing regional antinuclear sentiment directed at terminating the ANZUS alliance and U.S. regional military access.

The fringe includes Australian and New Zealand leftist trade unionists (some who have had links to Moscow through the World Federation of Trade Unions), a few parliamentarians, some academics and journalists, and various peace groups. With what became general public opposition to hosting anything nuclear, their objectives have been achieved in New Zealand, but they have little prospect for success in Australia.

The Australian government also worries that inadequate U.S. attention to the region can damage shared interests. That view was succinctly put by the Australian ambassador to the United States in 1985: "If you want the South Pacific to become an area where the Soviet Union, Cuba and others of that stripe can find fertile ground . . . on which they can develop activities directly prejudicial to our interest, then continue with a policy of indifference. . . . "[53] Those allusions hardly apply any longer, but the thrust of the argument remains intact.

New Zealand perceives fewer potential threats than does Australia and plays little in the way of a security role beyond its immediate island neighbors. That, coupled with a deeply rooted aversion to nuclear power, led Wellington to risk the United States–New Zealand leg of ANZUS by banning access to New Zealand by nuclear-armed or -powered ships. Given U.S. policy neither to confirm nor deny the presence of nuclear weapons on U.S. ships, New Zealand's actions had the practical effect of banning the entire U.S. Navy. The United States responded by suspending its ANZUS security obligations to New Zealand. Most forms of defense and intelligence cooperation and high-level official dialogue were also terminated. An unfortunate side effect was the demise of trilateral ANZUS dialogue and cooperation vis-à-vis shared regional interests.

The election of a National Party government in New Zealand in October 1990, followed by a relaxing of East-West relations, eased relations with the United States, as did President Bush's decision to remove tactical nuclear weapons from ships and aircraft and New Zealand's strong stand on behalf of the coalition effort in the Gulf crisis. The New Zealand government nevertheless faces serious political fallout should it choose to amend existing antinuclear legislation, and the fundamental difference with Washington remains.

The Australia–New Zealand ANZUS leg and the older bilateral "ANZAC" defense relationship remain intact, and Australia seeks to maintain strong defense cooperation links with New Zealand. Many Australians see New Zealand's reluctance to invest in defense as but one element in an uncharted drift by New Zealand toward pacifism and isolationism, though this has been tempered since New Zealand's Labour Party exited from office in 1990. Given New Zealand's considerable political influence in the region, especially in the Polynesian states, such a drift would have negative implications for broader Western regional interests. Both Labour and National New Zealand governments have denied the legitimacy of these concerns.

France

France, among the first to colonize the South Pacific, is the last major colonial presence in the South Pacific: New Caledonia, French Polynesia, and tiny Wallis and Futuna. Developments in those territories are addressed in chapter 3.

French national interests in the Pacific relate not to territorial resources but rather to perceptions of France's global role, the independent French nuclear deterrent, commitments to citizens of France in the Pacific, and the concept that the territories are parts of France—not colonies. For many in France, especially conservative forces, retaining France's remaining overseas possessions is an inseparable element of France's global role and influence. The French navy argues that global power projection requires the security of global sovereign port access.

While it has suspended its nuclear testing for 1992, France has repeatedly asserted that independent testing in

French Polynesia (as opposed to the British practice of testing in Nevada) is essential to France's independent nuclear capability. French Socialist governments have displayed flexibility with respect to the political evolution of French Pacific territories, but they are at one with the conservative parties in asserting that French Pacific nuclear testing is nonnegotiable; as mentioned, the French Socialist government has indicated it will not retain its suspension of testing unless other nuclear powers do likewise.

It is possible that France also views the Marquesas Islands in French Polynesia as potentially important to the European space program. The Marquesas, close to the equator, could be a geographically suitable alternative to politically problem-prone French Guiana as a site for the French space launch program.

From the broader perspective of Western interests, some French policies and activities in the Pacific have been a negative factor. The commencement of nuclear testing in French Polynesia in 1966 (U.S. Pacific testing ended in 1962) has been the primary catalyst for antinuclear sentiment not only in the islands but also in Australia and New Zealand. It can be plausibly argued that, absent French nuclear testing, the ANZUS alliance would have remained intact, and there would be no strong antinuclear movement, no South Pacific Nuclear Free Zone, and little pressure on U.S. Navy port access.

Kanak pressure for New Caledonia's independence and past French repressive measures in that territory have become the major regional decolonization issue. The conservative Chirac government's sanctioning of the bombing by French intelligence agents of the Greenpeace *Rainbow Warrior* in Auckland harbor in 1986 transformed regional resentment of France into regional outrage.[54] France had become the Pacific pariah.

Recognition of the foregoing, particularly the deteriorating New Caledonia situation, led to the 1988 changes in French Pacific territorial policy described in chapter 3. Earlier efforts of the previous Chirac government to build diplomatic bridges with island states have been intensified, in the main through new development assistance programs. These measures have been paralleled by strengthened French support of some regional institutions, particularly the South Pacific Commission, and by involvement of territorial leaders in the development of French regional policies (a point not lost on U.S. territorial leaders who are ignored in the formulation of U.S. regional policies).

France also is developing defense cooperation links with postcoup Fiji and for a time encouraged establishment of a Polynesian subregional grouping as a counterforce to the Melanesians who, in various regional forums, are the most critical of French territorial policies and nuclear testing. To some degree these and other French efforts designed to broaden existing cracks in regional cohesion have met with success. But French nuclear testing, if resumed, will continue to be a major regional issue. The ultimate future of the French territories, especially New Caledonia, also remains a question mark given efforts by Kanak and loyalist extremists to sabotage the Matignon Accords. No one doubts France's ability to maintain military control, but there is the question of political will should the cost become too high in financial and human terms.

Japan

Japanese strategic interests in the Pacific islands today parallel those of Australia and the United States, particularly the region's relationship to sea- and air lanes linking Japan with North America and with the mineral resources of Australia, Papua New Guinea, and New Caledonia that are essential to Japanese industry (for example, iron, coal, bauxite, copper, and nickel). Japan in turn is the major export partner and source of private investment capital for many island states and territories. The region also is a major source of Japan's tuna and other marine protein. Evolution of seabed mining technology and likely future demand for regional seabed mineral resources suggest a potential Japanese economic interest. Until recently, however, Tokyo paid little attention to the Pacific islands; it perceived no threats to limited Japanese interests and viewed the Pacific islands as the exclusive sphere of influence and responsibility of the United States (the North Pacific) and of Australia, New Zealand, and France (the South Pacific). Japanese activity thus was limited to modest aid programs, fisheries development, and private capital ventures.

Japanese relations with the region also have suffered from policies and actions that the island states strongly resented. Past Japanese proposals to dispose of nuclear and toxic wastes in the Pacific Ocean were considered a major threat to the region's marine resources. Driftnet fishing by Japanese fleets generated regionwide outrage but was terminated in 1990 after intense regional, U.S., and UN pressure. The island states also took umbrage at Japanese reluctance to enter into a regional fisheries agreement similar to that of the United States and Japan's past practice of using aid to promote Japanese commercial interests.

Japan's perceptions of its regional role began to change in the mid-1980s. There was emerging concern about Soviet inroads at a time when traditional aid donors could no longer satisfy regional expectations. There also was an accurate perception of growing regional frustration with high levels of dependence on traditional Western links and the related political impulse to explore alternatives. These developments coincided with pressure from the United States and others for Japan to engage in higher levels of development assistance burden-sharing as a palatable alternative to major increases in the proportion of Japanese GNP directed toward defense expenditures. In other words, Japan was, and remains, under pressure to contribute to Western security through development assistance that supports regional political stability in the Pacific and elsewhere.

Japan in the space of a few years has thus become the second largest source of South Pacific development assistance ($70 million in 1988 and $93.1 million in 1989 with further increases projected) and the largest for many South Pacific states other than Papua New Guinea. Tokyo has been cautious about translating its new regional role into political influence. Yet the influence that will inevitably follow argues for Japan's full integration into Western consultative processes relating to regional interests and challenges. The Japanese government already is informally exploring the possibility of membership in the South Pacific Commission.

The People's Republic of China (PRC)

First serious PRC interest in the Pacific islands emerged with regional decolonization in the 1970s and was spurred by concern about Soviet regional initiatives of that period. China started with no regional base, except for the presence of small Chinese communities in the region's major urban centers. In contrast to the ANZUS powers' strategic denial of Soviet efforts to establish a regional presence, there was little or no Western resistance to PRC embassies within the region, other political initiatives, and establishment of regional aid programs.

Chinese regional objectives related less to intrinsic regional interests than to broader strategic and political considerations, except for sporadic, limited interest in the region's marine resources. In particular, there was concern about Soviet "hegemonic" encirclement of China and about the possibility that Soviet regional successes could erode counterbalancing Western influence and military strength. Other objectives related to Taiwan's regional presence and "Third World solidarity." In that context, the following pattern of PRC objectives and regional policy themes emerged in the mid-1970s and was constant in the 1980s:

• establishment of diplomatic relationships with the region's island states
• demonstration of "Third World solidarity," including establishment of the diplomatic presence essential for Beijing's global and regional influence objectives

- blocking of Soviet diplomatic and other regional access
- diplomatic support for the ANZUS alliance, including subtle support for and encouragement of a Western military presence as a counter to Soviet military and hegemonic threats
- displacement or blocking of Taiwan's diplomatic and economic relationships
- establishment of small but highly visible aid programs intended to yield political influence.

An essential condition to Western and island state acceptance of a PRC regional presence was met in the early 1970s by Australia's and New Zealand's establishment of diplomatic relations with Beijing and President Nixon's China initiative leading to restored PRC-U.S. relationships. Chinese diplomatic relations with Fiji and Western Samoa followed in 1975, with Papua New Guinea in 1976, and with other regional states in the 1980s. Embassies were established in Fiji, Western Samoa, and Papua New Guinea in the 1970s and, more recently, in the Federated States of Micronesia. Though low profile, their diplomatic presence in the South Pacific was in fact greater than that of the United States until 1988. These developments were generally deliberate parallels to initial Soviet regional diplomatic initiatives.

Aid, technical assistance, cultural exchanges, and high-level official visits followed. Sports stadiums were constructed in Western Samoa and Papua New Guinea, as well as the parliament house in Vanuatu. There also have been multimillion-dollar interest-free loans ($8.25 million to Western Samoa alone in recent years), cash grants to key states, trade agreements (for example, purchase of Fiji sugar at a price well above market value), and technical assistance and training. Following Fiji's 1987 military coups, China provided medical teams to offset the loss of emigrating Indian medical specialists.

There also have been official visits to Beijing by regional prime ministers, foreign ministers, and other cabinet-level officials and reciprocal Chinese visits. The most notable of the latter was the 1985 regional tour of then Communist Party General Secretary Hu Yaobang who counseled his hosts on the perils of Soviet "hegemonism." The anti-Soviet comments of then Chinese Vice Premier Li Xiannian at a 1978 Beijing banquet honoring the visit of Fiji's prime minister, Ratu Sir Kamisese Mara, were sufficiently pointed to prompt the Soviet bloc diplomatic guests to walk out.[55]

Commitment to Third World solidarity prompted Beijing's early signing of the SPNFZ treaty protocols, but apparently with some misgivings. One influential Chinese scholar cautioned that measures such as SPNFZ can hurt Chinese security interests because a "neutral Pacific is a Soviet Pacific."[56] Beijing also has been unsympathetic to New Zealand's disruption of the ANZUS alliance. It has counseled island state governments against adoption of nuclear-free policies like those of Wellington.

Beijing has been less than successful in its efforts to displace or block Taiwan's presence. Four smaller island states – Nauru, the Solomons, Tonga, and Tuvalu – maintain diplomatic or consular relationships with Taiwan. Quasi-official Taiwan trade offices have been established in Papua New Guinea and Fiji. Several island states have been receptive to Taiwan's offers of aid and joint economic ventures.

The region's images of both Taipei and Beijing have suffered in the past several years. Taiwan's fishing fleets too frequently have poached tuna from island state EEZs and, like the Japanese, have engaged in driftnet fishing. Beijing, in turn, has suffered from regional reactions to the repression of the Chinese democracy movement.

Despite improvement in its relations with Moscow, Beijing is likely to continue its low-profile presence in the Pacific islands. But the limited influence of the Chinese may wane further as a consequence of Taiwanese inroads, unfavorable regional comparisons of Russian internal reform vis-à-vis Chinese domestic repression, and the evaporation of regional perceptions of a Soviet/Russian threat.

Taiwan's enormous foreign exchange reserves, related expanding technical and development assistance programs, and willingness to use these assets in the pursuit of political objectives suggest that Taiwan's presence may increase, especially in smaller states that are particularly aid dependent. As in the past, there also will be a continuing tendency for island state governments to take advantage of the competition between Taipei and Beijing. As one recent example, Fiji in early 1990 accepted a $2 million interest-free loan from Taiwan for the purchase of weaponry and then negotiated a $10 million interest-free PRC loan for construction of a convention center.

From a Western perspective, the Chinese presence in the Pacific islands, both Beijing's and Taipei's, has generally been a political plus and probably will remain so.

Other External Powers

Aside from the traditional Western presence and some Soviet/Russian, Chinese, and Japanese activities, a broad range of other external players is now active in the South Pacific. Some, like Great Britain and Germany, have interests paralleling those of the ANZUS powers, historic regional links, and major regional aid programs. Great Britain, through Commonwealth links with former colonies and a diplomatic presence throughout the region, still wields some political influence. Others, such as South Korea, pursue a narrow economic interest agenda. The remainder pursue a diverse range of objectives peculiar to equally diverse national interests.

The Indonesians have unique strategic and political regional interests. The only island state land border is that of Papua New Guinea with Indonesia's Irian Jaya Province on New Guinea island. Relations between the two states have been troubled for years by the border actions of the small Organisasi Papua Merdeka (OPM) indigenous separatist movement that seeks Irian Jaya's independence from Indonesia. Indonesian military efforts to suppress this rebellion have included many forays across the common land border. The OPM often has attempted to use Papua New Guinea as a sanctuary. In 1990, while operating in Papua New Guinea, it seized five hostages (including a U.S. missionary) and held them for several weeks. A related problem for Papua New Guinea is the presence of thousands of Irianese refugees and indigenous sympathy for insurrectionists who have ethnic, tribal, and cultural links to Papua New Guinea. Only political pragmatism and diplomatic restraint in both capitals have contained this situation, and cooperation between Indonesia and Papua New Guinea to deal with the border problem has improved considerably. The OPM issue is distracting and unwelcome to Papua New Guinea as well as Indonesia.

Australia and Papua New Guinea, as indicated earlier, share concern that reemergence of Sukarnoism in Jakarta could lead to military and political adventurism directed at Papua New Guinea. Indonesia, for its part, is concerned that chronic instability in Papua New Guinea could deteriorate to more threatening political chaos, associated violence, and support for the OPM insurrection. A June 1990 RAND Corporation report to the Department of Defense commented on this point:

> Indonesia's history reveals little tolerance of turmoil on its borders and a tendency to take action. Australia also would not be comfortable with such a situation near its borders, especially in a former colony in which it has sizable interests and attachments. Both countries might feel a need for action [with the consequence of military confrontation].[57]

Jakarta also has developed a political dialogue and some military links with Fiji. So has Malaysia, whom Papua New Guinea has recently welcomed as a defense program provider. These ASEAN and other new Asian linkages are actively pursued by Fiji and other island states as a strategy to diversify their diplomatic, political, and economic relationships. Papua New Guinea has subscribed to ASEAN's principles and holds observer status.

Cuba and Vietnam (particularly the former) developed a dialogue with, and occasional diplomatic presence in, Vanuatu. They were instrumental in Vanuatu's becoming a member of the Non-Aligned Movement. The Cubans offered police training and other instruction, while Vietnam has provided small medical assistance teams. These links have recently deteriorated, and Cuban and Vietnamese influence has fallen to little if any consequence. North Korea has established diplomatic relations with Vanuatu and a few other island states, and a number of island students (including from Papua New Guinea, Vanuatu, and New Caledonia) participated in the 1989 Pyongyang Thirteenth World Festival of Youths and Students. A recent RAND Corporation report cited information to the effect that eight people from New Caledonia remained in Pyongyang to attend a training camp where instructions may have included terrorist tactics, but such contacts have not been repeated.[58] Most North Korean efforts to establish dialogue with regional states have been rebuffed, although there is some contact with and support for a few radical elements in Papua New Guinea and elsewhere.

In the mid-1980s, Libya joined the strategic competition in the islands with funding and paramilitary training of factions in Vanuatu and New Caledonia and support of OPM elements in exile in Vanuatu. Before the factional strife in Vanuatu softened radical tendencies there, a Libyan diplomatic presence was being considered. Some radical elements of the Kanak independence movement in New Caledonia have strong ties with Libya; members of that faction were responsible for the 1989 assassination of Jean-Marie Tjibaou, the moderate Kanak leader. There also have been links to, and limited support of, some radical elements in Papua New Guinea and in French Polynesia. Most Libyan South Pacific activity has been orchestrated by the Libyan *Mathaba* (Anti-Imperialism Center) and by the Libyan People's Bureau in Kuala Lumpur. Mischief making for the West in general and France in particular appears to have been Libya's motive. Libyan interest and activity in the region has fallen off in the past several years and has virtually ended in Vanuatu.

Israel's diplomatic presence, aid, and technical assistance programs are a minor element in its broader global strategy of building influence and support as it competes with the Arab world. Israel's focus on Fiji relates to the latter's major participation in peacekeeping forces in Lebanon and the Sinai.

India has a direct interest in Fiji because of the latter's large ethnic Indian community, nearly half the total population. Although New Delhi currently has little influence in the region, India's expanding naval and other capabilities, as well as broader leadership ambitions, could lead to a more active regional role. Some observers have commented that, if Fiji were in the Indian Ocean, there would inevitably have been Indian military intervention following Fiji's first military coup in 1987. There have been allegations that Indian intelligence officers were associated with large-scale smuggling of arms and other military gear into Fiji in 1988. India's ambassador to Fiji was expelled by Suva in 1990 following accusations of interference in Fiji's internal affairs. One consequence of the deteriorating relationship between Fiji and India was Pakistan's extension of some military training to Fiji.

Thus far, at worst, the activities of some secondary external players such as Libya have been a major nuisance while those of the more constructive players, particularly Britain and Germany, are a significant plus for both regional and Western interests. Taken together, these secondary influences complicate the islands' diplomatic and political tapestry and require more dialogue and coordination between major Western players. But they also offer small regional states alternatives to the narrow range of traditional influences.

8

The Soviet Union and
the Pacific Islands

Although the Soviet Union was the West's only significant competitor in the Pacific islands after World War II,
much of that competition had been more potential than
real. The free association relationship between the United
States and North Pacific Micronesian states, and U.S. territorial and commonwealth relationships with Guam and the
Northern Mariana Islands, ensured no Soviet military access in the North Pacific islands and limited potential for
political access. The political inclinations of South Pacific
island states blocked Soviet military access and inhibited
political influence within the island region. Change and turmoil in the Soviet Union, foreign policy reform, the end of
the cold war, and the eventual collapse of the USSR as a
national entity, with its replacement by very different poli-
ties, reduced and then essentially removed any challenge to
Western interests.

Traditional Soviet Regional
Interests and Objectives[59]

The Pacific islands undoubtedly were the lowest of Soviet
priorities within the Asia-Pacific region. Moreover, unlike

Western powers active in the Pacific islands, the Soviet Union pursued its regional objectives from a zero base: no territorial presence, no resident diplomatic representation, no military presence, no ideological affinity, no investment links, and insignificant trade levels.

Before the mid-1970s, Moscow's regionally related activities were limited to verbal attacks in the United Nations and elsewhere on regional decolonization processes and objectives (particularly those relating to the Trust Territory of the Pacific Islands), intensive hydrographic and oceanographic research related to marine resources and submarine warfare requirements, intelligence collection directed at the Kwajalein Missile Range facility and French nuclear testing, and encouragement of regional antinuclear emotions directed at French nuclear testing and U.S. Navy port access. A coherent set of regional policy objectives and a related strategy for the Pacific islands began to emerge only in the mid-1970s. By 1985 there was a clear pattern of Soviet objectives in, or related to, the Pacific islands:

- Western and regional state acceptance of the Soviet Union as a Pacific power with legitimate regional interests
- erosion of Western influence and promotion of island state nonalignment
- restraints on U.S. military capabilities through politically inspired means aimed at restricting U.S. regional port and air access
- related to the foregoing, opposition to the free association relationship between elements of the former Trust Territory of the Pacific Islands and the United States
- establishment of a resident diplomatic presence in the Pacific islands
- access to regional marine resources (particularly tuna) and to commercial shipping and trade opportunities. The Soviets were interested in participating in any future development of regional seabed mineral resources, and the successor state of Russia may well continue that interest.

With the exception of access to regional fisheries, the potential for seabed minerals mining, and shipping and trade opportunities, all of the Soviet objectives related to global East-West competition, Soviet interests in the broader Asia-Pacific region, and Moscow's determination to advance the reality of the Soviet Union as a global power through a corollary presence and influence in all global regions.

Connected to that point, some broader Asia-Pacific objectives related directly either to Western interests in the Pacific islands or to Soviet regional strategies. These included

• reduction of Western naval superiority in the Pacific through naval arms control agreements
• erosion of Australian and New Zealand commitment to the ANZUS alliance (an objective largely achieved in New Zealand, although not a direct consequence of Soviet action)
• termination of U.S. access to defense facilities in the Philippines.

The Emerging Soviet Presence

"On-the-ground" Soviet pursuit of regional objectives began in 1976 with proposals to establish a Soviet embassy in Tonga, a fisheries fleet base in the same state, Aeroflot access for crew exchanges and resupply, and Soviet construction of a dock and expansion of Tonga's major airport. (The Soviet Union had already established diplomatic relations with many key island states, including Tonga, but with nonresident diplomatic representation based in Wellington and Canberra.) Tongan conservatism and suspicion, and Australian and New Zealand pressure, ensured the proposal's failure. Ironically, New Zealand in 1978 provided to the Soviet Union that which it had counseled Tonga against: a fisheries agreement with shore access and limited related facilities. The application of a double standard did not go unnoticed in the Pacific islands.

The Tonga episode triggered a major reassessment by Canberra and Wellington of Soviet regional ambitions. Two consequences were (1) expansion of Australia's and New Zealand's regional diplomatic presence and development assistance programs (Australia quadrupled its aid programs in the region), and (2) pressure on Washington to play a more active secondary role in the South Pacific. That pressure generated Washington decisions in 1977 and 1978 to establish a small regional development assistance program, new educational and cultural exchange programs, and the first coherent Pacific islands policy. If nothing else, the "Russians are coming" syndrome had focused new ANZUS interest on the South Pacific.

The three ANZUS capitals agreed that Soviet efforts to establish a regional presence would be countered by increases in development assistance, trade promotion, and promotion of strengthened regional institutions. Australia and New Zealand would continue to play the lead alliance role in the South Pacific, but the United States would strengthen its supportive role. The United States would continue to play the lead Western role in its traditional area of presence and influence: the Micronesian islands of the North Pacific.

Pre-Gorbachev Soviet efforts to establish a diplomatic presence in other states and to conclude fisheries or trade arrangements were all rebuffed, at least in part because of regional reactions to the Soviet invasion of Afghanistan in 1979, but also because of crude, ideologically oriented diplomacy that did not appeal to conservative island state governments. Early Soviet efforts to penetrate the region also were hampered by ignorance, including a tendency to interpret all regional political developments and issues in the context of East-West competition. The Soviets had a marginal measure of regional access, starting in the late 1970s, through Soviet cruise ships operating under charter to Australian tour organizations. Even these arrangements were terminated for several years as one response to the Soviet invasion of Afghanistan. More recently, with major expansion of the Soviet merchant marine, the latter became a factor in Pacific island trade.

A classic implementation of the ANZUS decision to deny any form of Soviet access to the region occurred in 1980. The Soviet Academy of Sciences had offered the regional Committee for the Coordination of Joint Prospecting for Mineral Resources in the South Pacific (now the South Pacific Applied Geoscience Commission) a five-year marine resource research project involving two annual research cruises and port access throughout the Pacific islands. The offer was accepted, but then rejected following dialogue between the ANZUS partners and a counteroffer of a similar project. Washington, Canberra, and Wellington were concerned with three dimensions of the Soviet project: the potential military applications of the research, the potential for political meddling flowing from port access, and the precedent of any form of Soviet regional access.

Parallel to the foregoing initiatives, Soviet South Pacific hydrographic/oceanographic research, begun in 1957, intensified. Surveillance of the Kwajalein Missile Range facility and French nuclear testing also increased throughout this period and continued. The surveillance apparently included entry into Kwajalein's lagoon to steal missile flight recorders. According to a *New York Times* report, five U.S. searches in July 1987 of the lagoon failed to locate a recorder but did turn up a Soviet sailor's hat, Russian vodka bottles, packs of Russian cigarettes, and Soviet-produced bug repellent![60]

Another, continuing dimension of Soviet regional activity was intensification of "disinformation" relating to U.S. military planning for and activities in Micronesia, especially Palau. In the political arena, penetration efforts increased with invitations to island students, trade union leaders, and antinuclear activists to visit the Soviet Union for conferences, education, or short-term training.

The Gorbachev Era and
Regional Turning Points

The beginning of the Gorbachev era in 1985 coincided with regional developments that provided new opportunities and a more positive atmosphere for Soviet initiatives. Generational change in the region's political leadership was foremost among these factors. The first generation of postcolonial leaders was being replaced by new elites who were generally better educated, less conservative, more nationalistic, assertive, and often more resentful of aid dependency on and related political influence by a narrow range of traditional Western donors. Still conservative by most Third World standards, these emerging elites are nonetheless more prone to experiment with new international links—if only to demonstrate independent foreign policies and to diversify economic dependency.

In more recent years, global change in East-West relations, reform and turmoil within the Soviet Union, the Soviet withdrawal from Afghanistan, and Moscow's tolerance of democratization in Eastern Europe became major factors in eroding traditional suspicion of Moscow's objectives and activities.

The election of Labor governments in Australia and New Zealand in 1983 and 1984 gave new life to regional sentiment for a nuclear-free zone and termination of French nuclear testing. The 1986 Treaty of Rarotonga establishing the South Pacific Nuclear Free Zone was one major consequence. Washington's failure to sign the treaty protocols contrasted sharply with accession by the Soviet Union; regional leaders welcomed Moscow's action. Separately, the New Zealand Labor government in early 1985 implemented its nuclear-free policies, which in 1987 were enshrined in legislation. The United States responded by suspending its ANZUS obligations to and defense cooperation with New Zealand. Moscow applauded New Zealand's action and cited it as an appropriate precedent for Australia and the island states.

During the same time, Kanak pressures for New Caledonian independence began to peak, eliciting repressive responses from the then-conservative government in Paris. Regional outrage intensified with the 1985 French bombing of the Greenpeace ship *Rainbow Warrior* in Auckland harbor, an act of state terrorism by anyone's definition. The tardiness and softness of Washington's reaction to that incident, a perception that the United States had not signed the SPNFZ treaty protocols because it supported French nuclear testing, and a perception of U.S. tolerance for French repressive measures in New Caledonia played into Moscow's hands. These perceptions were reinforced by Soviet disinformation and by visiting Soviet diplomats.

Against the background of the fisheries jurisdiction dispute between regional states and the United States, in 1985 Kiribati concluded a fisheries agreement with the Soviet Union. The agreement provided Soviet fishing fleet access to Kiribati's exclusive economic zone for an annual fee of US$1.5 million. The agreement did not include shore access by either Soviet trawlers or Aeroflot. The Soviet payment represented about 15 percent of Kiribati's budget, obviously a significant inducement. The ANZUS governments, but Canberra in particular, were concerned not only about the general precedent of formalized Soviet regional access with its political implications, but also about shore access, which, if provided later, would offer opportunities for political meddling. Canberra and Wellington thus actively opposed the Kiribati agreement, while Washington counseled caution in dealing with the Soviets.

A senior U.S. defense official also publicly expressed concern for the potential establishment of ground-based intelligence facilities directed at Kwajalein, others that could benefit Soviet military satellite programs, Pacific missile testing, or new Soviet air routes to Central America.[61] These concerns, with good cause, were considered less than credible by regional governments.

A similar fisheries agreement was concluded with Vanuatu in 1987, but it provided for periodic trawler shore access for resupply and crew rest. Both agreements were aborted after their first year when the Soviets argued that the tuna catch was not economic and insisted upon fee reductions. One knowledgeable Australian source estimates that the Kiribati agreement netted a catch valued at only US$1.7 million, while the overall annual cost of fleet operations had been the equivalent of about US$15 million. The Soviets' Vanuatu venture apparently was not cost-effective either.[62]

For the longer term, both agreements may have been politically productive for the Soviets in that their performance eased concern that they would fish for more than tuna. Most observers now agree that the Soviets adhered meticulously to the agreements and did not engage in any untoward activities. Foreign Minister Shevardnadze, during a 1987 visit to Canberra, confirmed that expanded Soviet political influence was an anticipated benefit of "establishment of commercial ties with the islands."[63] After the Vanuatu agreement was terminated, the Soviets explored possibilities with Fiji and the Solomons and in 1990 concluded a fisheries agreement with Papua New Guinea, providing for the stationing of two Soviet trawlers in Papua New Guinea waters, shore access, and fisheries technical and marketing assistance.

In 1990, five years after the conclusion of the first Soviet fisheries agreement, considerable evidence indicates that this form of penetration of the South Pacific was never an element of Soviet grand strategy for the region. The Soviet Union's most prominent regional specialist, Dr. Viktor Vrevsky, asserted in late 1990 that the Soviet Fisheries Ministry had launched its regional initiatives without any coordination with the Foreign Ministry and that "we had no capability or valid reason to be there except for showing the flag."[64] Similar comments, and resentment of the absence of cost-effectiveness of South Pacific fisheries operations, were offered to the author by various Soviet Foreign Ministry officials during a mid-1990 visit to Moscow. Ironically, the background of Papua New Guinea's new fisheries agreement with Moscow appears to have come about under equally confused circumstances. The agreement was opposed by Papua New Guinea Fisheries Minister Allan Ebu as providing "zero economic benefit" to his country. He also has said that his government had "pressed" Moscow to sign the agreement! The agreement was advocated by Foreign Minister Michael Somare and supported by a majority of his cabinet colleagues. It seems likely that Somare and others saw the agreement primarily as an effective device to diversify international ties. They may also have been seeking to demonstrate, especially to Canberra, their country's independence in the area of foreign affairs.[65]

Coincident with Soviet fisheries successes, the Soviet Union signaled new political, economic, and security interest in the Asia-Pacific region, including the Pacific islands, via Gorbachev's 1986 Vladivostok speech and subsequent statements in Krasnoyarsk and elsewhere. In one form or another, explicitly or implicitly, traditional Soviet regional interests and objectives were reaffirmed. Any focus on ideological competition was eliminated, however, and there was a new emphasis on political and economic pragmatism. As with Soviet foreign policy generally, diplomacy in the Pacific islands became more knowledgeable, conciliatory, and less confrontational—and thus far more effective. Soviet officials visiting island states stressed that there were no "evil intentions" behind the development of "normal relations," a point also emphasized by the Soviet Union to Australia and New Zealand because of these countries' regional strategic concerns.

Of more fundamental importance, the Soviet Union established a fresh set of priorities in the last stages of its existence as a national entity. It sought integration into the mainstream of Asia-Pacific political and economic processes with the hope of participating in the region's economic boom. Related to that objective, it also sought Australian, Asian, and U.S. investment in the development of the Soviet Far East and participation in regional organizations. Beyond these new regional objectives, the goal of reducing East-West tensions was to allow the Soviets to reduce their military budget. Taken together, these new priorities mandated a more cautious pursuit of traditional objectives inimical to Western or regional state interests.

New sophistication in Soviet regional diplomacy also reflected "new thinking" in Third World policies, including shifts away from doctrinaire ideological approaches and emphasis of support for Marxist-Leninist regimes toward more active pursuit of relationships with and influence in a broader range of developing countries. According to this new thinking, particular attention was to be given to states, even though they may be on a capitalist course, that had grievances with the United States and other Western powers. One Soviet official commented that the West's tendency to act "crudely" or "brazenly" in Third World countries produced reactions that made cooperation with Moscow especially attractive.[66]

The application of these principles was illustrated in part by regional diplomacy that continued to focus on nuclear concerns (for example, French nuclear testing and the British, French, and U.S. failure to adhere to the SPNFZ treaty protocols), French Pacific colonial policies, the Palau issue, island state frustration with aid dependency, a related search for diversification of economic links, and regional concerns about becoming enmeshed in superpower rivalry and potential conflict. The new importance that Moscow attached to strengthened political and economic relations with Australia, coupled with recognition of Canberra's sensitivities about Soviet activities in the South Pacific, ensured new Soviet restraint in acting upon these opportunities.

Implementation of new thinking and pursuit of related traditional objectives included a surge, in the late 1980s, of visits by Soviet officials and delegations seeking not only new fisheries agreements, but also establishment of diplomatic missions, cultural exchanges, economic joint ventures, and new trade relationships. Invitations to regional political leaders to visit the Soviet Union became more frequent. There were offers of scholarships, short-term training, and conference participation. These activities, however, seem to have diminished after 1989. That development apparently stemmed from Moscow's perception of marginal return, the deepening economic crisis faced by the Soviet Union, new pressures on already scarce hard currency resources, and preoccupation with internal political turmoil. The major success in this new drive for closer regional relationships and a related diplomatic presence was the opening in early 1990 of a Soviet embassy in Port Moresby, Papua New Guinea.

Soviet Disinformation

Soviet tactics exposed some inconsistencies. While seeking improved relations with the United States, Moscow continued disinformation campaigns directed at U.S. regional activities. Recent cases included a 1988 disinformation program directed at linking the United States to the 1987 military coups in Fiji.[67] There also was continuing Soviet disinformation directed at U.S. political and defense objectives related to Palau and the Micronesian states in free association with the United States, although at a lower level than in preceding years.[68] Although these activities were in conflict with a Soviet commitment to halt disinformation directed at the United States, it is not clear whether they were deliberate or were only a reflection of Moscow's own distorted perceptions of the region and of U.S. defense planning. Soviet officials in Moscow in 1990 told the author that any current disinformation activities reflected "bureaucratic inertia" rather than current Soviet policy.[69] A leading Soviet regional specialist described past disinformation on U.S. policies and activity in Micronesia as "nothing else but elements of the Cold War period."[70]

Soviet Surrogate Activities

The regional activities of Soviet front organizations, regional surrogates, and others who pursued objectives congruent with those of Moscow had a regional impact. Their primary regional causes were termination of the ANZUS alliance and of the joint defense facilities in Australia; promotion of a nuclear-free Pacific (including termination of U.S. regional naval and other military access and of French nuclear testing); promotion of France's political departure from the South Pacific through independence for New Caledonia and French Polynesia; and opposition to U.S. defense relationships with Palau and the Micronesian states in free association with the United States. Regional political and environmental concerns, such as New Caledonia's political future and French nuclear testing, provided fertile ground for the activities of these groups.[71]

During its existence, the World Federation of Trade Unions (WFTU) was foremost among regionally active Soviet fronts. It operated primarily through Marxist and other leftist Australian trade unions and their leaders and the Marxist-led New Zealand Council of Trade Unions (NZCTU). The NZCTU's president, Ken Douglas, also was active in the Moscow-oriented New Zealand Socialist Unity party. A number of leftist Australian and New Zealand unions were affiliated with the WFTU's industry secretariats and regularly participated in WFTU conferences. Some trade unions in New Caledonia, the Solomons, and Vanuatu affiliated with the WFTU.[72] Most of the region's unions were affiliated with the WFTU's free world counterpart: the International Confederation of Free Trade Unions (ICFTU).

The WFTU, at its 1978 Prague Conference, decided to place a greater focus on the South Pacific. The Pacific Trade Union Forum, later the Pacific Trade Union Community (PTUC), was established in 1980 and was dominated from the outset by Australian and New Zealand leftists who pressed a political agenda having everything to do with Soviet regional strategic and political objectives and little relationship to traditional labor concerns. Fijian PTUC activists were a significant component in the Fiji coalition government elected to office in 1987 that was deposed shortly afterward by a military coup. The coalition government had contemplated adopting nuclear-free policies similar to those of New Zealand.

The AFL-CIO and moderate Australian and New Zealand trade union leaders in 1982 sought to counter these influences by establishing the Labor Committee for Pacific Affairs. The effort foundered as a consequence of inadequate funding, inept American handling of visits by island trade union leaders to the United States, and a successful campaign by Australian and New Zealand leftists to discredit the committee with (false) allegations of CIA involvement. The AFL-CIO-backed Asia-American Free Labor Institute also opened an office in Suva, Fiji, and offered training and other labor-related programs that were well received in the region. That effort also largely foundered as a consequence of inadequate funding and (false) allegations of CIA backing.

Other Soviet front organizations active in the region included the World Peace Council, the Congress for International Cooperation and Disarmament, and the World Federation of Democratic Youth. Although not a Soviet front, the World Council of Churches and its regional affiliate, the Pacific Conference of Churches (PCC), had a proclivity to manipulate legitimate regional concerns in ways that focused exclusively on Western interests and behavior and had the practical effect of Soviet surrogacy. As one example, calls were made for the closure of U.S. Pacific bases and for denial of U.S. Navy access to regional ports, but no mention was made of Soviet Pacific forces. The PCC's influence declined some in recent years, mainly because of dissatisfaction with its political agenda on the part of some regional churches and a consequent reduction in its funding.

Antinuclear peace groups in Australia and New Zealand, often with links to and support from leftist trade unions, independently pursued objectives paralleling Moscow's, with no tolerance of Western strategies to deter conflict. Closely associated with similar groups in the Pacific islands, their primary causes paralleled those of the PTUC, including advocacy of unilateral disarmament. Progress in arms control agreements and the end of the cold war eroded the membership and zeal of regional peace groups.

Of considerable influence within Australia and New Zealand, but also to some degree within the Pacific islands, are some Australian and New Zealand leftist or otherwise anti-U.S. television journalists who have provided a steady flow of "documentaries" and other reporting sympathetic to Pacific peace group causes. Much of their data can be traced back to Soviet disinformation. Of greater significance in the island states has been the presence of leftist or pacifist U.S., Australian, and New Zealand faculty members in regional tertiary educational institutions (especially the University of the South Pacific in Fiji) from whence many of the Pacific islands' political elites emerged in the 1970s and 1980s.

In assessing these activities, it is important not to exaggerate their influence. But the latter became greater than might be expected, if only because of the inadequacy of counterbalancing political activism. A prominent Australian trade unionist, Michael Easson, points out that the PTUC until recently was the only major forum for regional union conferences and regional meetings of Pacific union leaders and that it set the agenda for many regional issues.[73] Easson also makes the point that moderate labor forces tended to concede the South Pacific to the left through neglect.[74]

The extent of direct Soviet involvement in all of the foregoing is difficult to document. The Soviet role in WFTU activities was clear and direct, as were the activities of Moscow-oriented Australian and New Zealand Marxists. The Soviet ambassador was expelled from New Zealand in 1980 for financing activities of the Moscow-oriented Socialist Unity Party whose leaders were active in the NZCTU and PTUC. In August 1987, Australia's then foreign minister, Bill Hayden, commented: "There is a surprisingly high level of Soviet-backed activities in South Pacific countries." He went on to say that Australian intelligence reports showed that the Soviets are recruiting and funding local activists, primarily through third parties.[75]

Recent developments in Eastern Europe brought about a major diminution of front and surrogate activities in the Pacific islands. The WFTU, as a consequence of that change, was significantly weakened, as were other front organizations. Paralleling these developments, the ICFTU, in collaboration with regional unions, established the South Pacific and Oceanic Council of Trade Unions (SPOCTU) in 1990. SPOCTU offers a more traditional and less political agenda of labor issues and provides a range of needed services to regional unions, including training. Simultaneously with the formation of SPOCTU, the PTUC dissolved itself, but the course of SPOCTU's appeal remained uncertain.

The Military Dimension

Although the end of the cold war is a reality, so is the inheritance of the formidable buildup of Soviet Pacific naval and air power over the past twenty years. What was the Soviet Pacific fleet is still the largest of the Russian Navy's four fleets. The political conversion of the Soviet Union to the Commonwealth of Independent States, and to Russia in particular, has not yet been matched by change in these capabilities. In 1989, the Department of Defense expected that these naval forces would be reduced with retirement of a number of aging submarines and destroyers and replacement by fewer ships – but that overall capabilities would be enhanced through modernization.[76]

Western, particularly U.S., Pacific air and naval assets nonetheless generally remain quantitatively and qualitatively superior to those of Russia. The latter would be hard-pressed to sustain naval operations distant from Far Eastern waters, with one major exception applicable to the South Pacific. Russia has the capability to conduct mine warfare, including in the Strait of Malacca and Indonesian straits linking the Pacific and Indian Oceans, and to conduct antishipping submarine warfare throughout the Pacific. The Russian Air Force and naval aviation also could interdict shipping and allied naval forces throughout much of the north Pacific from bases in the Soviet Far East. With these exceptions, most Western defense analysts agree that Russian Pacific naval and air capabilities are best suited for protecting the Sea of Okhotsk base of the Russian Pacific Fleet's twenty-six strategic missile submarines. As for Cam Ranh Bay in Vietnam, the possibility of its survival in any major conflict would be bleak, and even that point is by now moot. The Russians have phased out their Cam Ranh operations.

There is no more Soviet Union. The new Russian state, operating on a democratic basis, is preoccupied with desperately needed socioeconomic domestic reforms. It looks to the West for sympathy and assistance and disclaims intentions to revive cold war competition, or indeed many of the Soviet Union's former external objectives. How this in time will crystallize into a coherent Russian foreign and defense policy in the Pacific remains to be seen. In the meantime, it is useful to trace the moderating trends evinced by the Soviet Union in its later stages, as possible lines of continuity.

Given the disparity between Soviet/Russian and Western Pacific naval assets and economic and technological restraints that ensured a continuing imbalance in those forces, a primary Soviet strategic objective was Pacific naval arms control agreements that would reduce Western naval superiority. Soviet initiatives in this area had little appeal in Washington and Tokyo.[77] Although the Soviet Union was and Russia remains essentially a land-based power with few overseas defense commitments, the United States is a maritime power linked to Asian and Pacific allies and trading partners by trans-Pacific sea- and air lanes. Five of the seven U.S. security alliances are with Asia-Pacific states, and nearly half of all U.S. foreign trade transits the Pacific.

A grudging Soviet recognition developed that U.S. Pacific forces carried regional missions unrelated to the Soviet Union and that they played a positive balancing, or stabilizing, role in Southeast and Northeast Asia that could serve some Soviet interests. Recognition, however, did not translate into acceptance of existing U.S. force levels or of their regional bases in Japan and the Philippines. Soviet officials also pressed the concept of "equal security" in the South Pacific in an attempt to encourage island states to see their security interests as being best served by excluding both superpowers – in reality the United States in the absence of any present or likely future Soviet military access.[78] Such a theme was pressed by Gorbachev in his 1986 Vladivostok speech, and in his 1987 *Merdeka* press interview. He described "mutual renunciation" of naval exercises and maneuvers as a model that could be extended to the South Pacific.[79] In short, the Soviets pressed for the reverse of the ANZUS objective of strategic denial: strategic denial of the region to the West in general and the United States in particular.

A particular Soviet concern, frequently expressed to the author by Soviet officials and academic regional specialists in Moscow in 1990, was the perception that the United States intended to build a major military basing complex in Micronesia (mainly in Palau and the Northern Mariana Islands), especially if the United States lost access to defense facilities in the Philippines. That perception was based in part on Soviet digestion of their own disinformation and that of regional peace groups, but it was also a product of U.S. official statements of the 1970s and early 1980s when such options were actively contemplated. Today, there is no such intent, even with the loss of access to the Philippines.[80] But the concern persisted. Moscow's agreement in late 1990 to a UN Security Council resolution approving termination of the trusteeship for the Northern Mariana Islands, the Federated States of Micronesia, and the Marshall Islands, required advance high-level official (but informal) assurances of no U.S. intent to build major new defense facilities in these islands.[81]

Meanwhile, though possessing a peacetime capability to project naval power into the South Pacific, the Soviets with rare exception refrained from such action. Nor did they seek naval port access or any land-based military facilities. The Soviet first deputy chief of naval operations, Vice Adm. Dmitry Komarov, in 1988 asserted that Soviet ships "rarely if ever exercise their right to freedom of navigation in the South Pacific." Also: "In the South Pacific one can only meet research vessels of the Soviet Navy . . . and also training ships that make voyages with cadets on board. We simply do not need to send our warships there."[82] Soviet Foreign Minister Shevardnadze, during a 1988 visit to Fiji, also asserted no Soviet interest in South Pacific military access.

Aside from the fact that no island state was likely to grant such access, Moscow calculated that the absence of Soviet naval activity in the South Pacific lowered regional threat perceptions and thus encouraged the notion that ANZUS and a regional U.S. military presence were not relevant to regional security – and could be a liability in the event of East-West conflict. A parallel calculation was that Soviet naval or other military activity in the South Pacific would be counterproductive vis-à-vis higher priority strategic objectives: Pacific naval arms control agreements, denial of regional U.S. Navy port access, improved relations with Australia and erosion of the latter's commitment to ANZUS, and island state nonalignment.

Western Responses

ANZUS's strategic denial of any form of Soviet regional access and influence succeeded through the mid-1980s until the end of the Soviet Union. The first Soviet successes – the early fisheries agreements – were a consequence of numerous regional factors, including resentment of a Western double standard. New Zealand and the United States both had fisheries agreements with the Soviet Union, including provision for shore access. That factor, together with the

Soviet track record in Kiribati and Vanuatu and a subsequent major Australian trade and fisheries agreement with the Soviet Union, eroded the credibility of Western counsel against such agreements. The West also came to accept that the Soviets, at least during the Gorbachev era, could have regional objectives—particularly that of access to marine resources—that posed no threat as long as they were not commingled with political mischief making. More recently, Washington, Canberra, and Wellington became relatively more relaxed about the 1990 opening of a Soviet embassy in Port Moresby. At the same time, they provided counsel to the Papua New Guinea government on the problems of coping with an inevitable KGB presence.

Changing regional and Western attitudes toward a Soviet presence were also characterized by new cooperation in marine resource-related oceanographic/hydrographic research. Past rejection of Soviet offers of cooperation had been replaced by tentative moves toward cooperation in this area. A current project, involving the Soviet Academy of Sciences ship *Mstislev Keldysh*, the South Pacific Applied Geoscience Commission, and Australian, New Zealand, and U.S. scientists, is researching hydrothermal vents in the ocean floor. The data will help identify seabed mineral resources. Fiji and Tonga, accepting counsel from Canberra and Wellington, altered past policies to permit port access for the research vessel.

The most significant Western response thus was to abandon total strategic denial of the Soviets. This was partially an acceptance of reality and partially a result of changing East-West relations. A Soviet diplomatic, trade, and fisheries presence was accepted, and strategic denial was limited to military access, intelligence activities, and political meddling.

Former Australian Prime Minister Robert Hawke and Foreign Minister Gareth Evans noted that it was unrealistic to attempt to insulate the South Pacific from all Soviet influences. They pointed out that total opposition to a Soviet regional role would be counterproductive, especially in the face of Australian and other Western "warming" of relationships with Moscow. They also argued that the Soviet Union should be "drawn into" the Pacific community in the absence of sound evidence of "Soviet malevolence." These statements were paralleled by expressions of concern about the lack of "transparency" of Soviet regional objectives, interest, and activities, and most Australian political leaders remained skeptical about Soviet assurances. The Australian government put Moscow on notice that only "normal," or "conventional," diplomatic behavior would be tolerated.[83] The New Zealand government viewed the emerging Soviet regional presence in much the same fashion as Canberra, but it was more cautious in its public statements.

Future Prospects

Most island state governments currently remain conservative and pragmatic. They have throughout been cautious about Soviet initiatives and motives. Although some island governments may have deliberately played the "Soviet card" to extract higher levels of Western sensitivity and development assistance, by and large there was remarkable restraint. From an island state perspective, the Soviets had little to offer in the way of things tangible other than hard currency payments for fisheries access, possibly modest trade, and marine resource–related oceanographic research. Even with the Soviet Union's meticulous adherence to the terms of its fisheries agreements with Kiribati and Vanuatu, several island states rejected more recent Soviet offers.

There also were self-imposed Soviet restraints. The Pacific islands were not a high priority. Consequently, the Soviet Union was reluctant to apply scarce hard currency to regional objectives. That limitation was exacerbated by the Soviet Union's economic crisis and by the distractions of internal change and turmoil. Even without these restraints, major political or military adventurism within the region was generally regarded as counterproductive vis-à-vis the Soviets' higher priority strategic and political objectives.

Confirming much of the above, Soviet officials and academic regional specialists described Soviet regional activities (or the lack thereof) for the foreseeable future as follows:[84]

• Moscow would be unlikely to try to establish additional embassies in the region in the immediate future because of economic constraints. Moscow recognized that most island state governments would seek Soviet commitments to aid or subsidized trade in exchange for diplomatic relations. There also was a new concern for Australian sensitivities regarding an overplayed Soviet hand.

• The future of Russian tuna fishing in the central Pacific may be in question. The Soviet experience entailed massive operational expenditures for a very modest economic return. Some Soviet officials and academic regional specialists urged that these operations end and that Soviet fishing fleets focus on the cold waters of the Pacific that they knew best. A new constraint became the cessation of subsidies for Soviet/Russian fisheries operations and a consequent requirement that they be cost-effective. On the other hand, Soviet officials recently explored the possibility of a regional fisheries agreement with the South Pacific Forum Fisheries Agency, presumably on the assumption that such an agreement could be more cost-effective than bilateral arrangements. Dr. Viktor Vrevsky, the Soviet regional specialist, normally was highly critical of Soviet fisheries agreements with Pacific island states. In late 1990, however, he said that, during an informal meeting with the vice president of the Federated States of Micronesia, he had "found that fisheries relations could be established" with that state.[85]

• Few trade opportunities are perceived, except on a limited basis in Papua New Guinea and perhaps Fiji. A barter arrangement exchanging Papua New Guinea coffee for Soviet helicopters was concluded in 1990.

• Opportunities for joint ventures in the islands appear limited mainly to fish processing. Even in this area there is an assumption that Russia will have difficulty competing with Japan and Taiwan. The Soviets in 1988 explored the possibility of a hardwood timber joint venture with Papua New Guinea.

• Moscow may consider establishment of small aid projects, but these probably would be limited to the transfer of human skills. They may be linked to existing regional organization or UN Development Program projects to minimize hard currency costs.

• Regional marine research will continue at a fairly high level, but with new efforts to cooperate with regional organizations. Cooperation with Western and regional state scientists will be welcomed. (Although much past Soviet Pacific marine research related to military capabilities, most current research seems to be directed at marine and seabed resources. There apparently is little parallel research on seabed mining technology. This suggests the possibility of marrying Western seabed mining technology with Russian seabed mineral resource data in joint ventures.)

The Soviet Union in its closing stages appears to have been reluctant to embarrass France with respect to its problems in New Caledonia or to seek political advantage from Papua New Guinea's internal problems related to the Bougainville secessionist movement. This flowed not only from Moscow's new regional priorities, but also from a perception of parallels with the Soviet Union's Baltic state problems. The Soviet perception of a parallel between France's ten-year self-determination plan for New Caledonia and Moscow's call for delays in that process in the Baltic states was cited by President Gorbachev in press conferences in Ottawa and in Washington, D.C., in June 1990.[86] Soviet officials also noted the ethnic population parallel of the large French settler presence in New Caledonia. Regarding Bougainville, Soviet officials in Moscow commented to the author on the parallel between Papua New

Guinea's "blockade" of that island as a secession response and early Soviet responses to the Lithuanian declaration of independence.

That the Soviets agreed in late 1990 to the UN Security Council acceptance of termination of the Micronesian trusteeship agreement resulted mainly from the end of the cold war and from Moscow's need for improved relations with the United States and Asia-Pacific states. That agreement required a direct approach to Foreign Minister Shevardnadze. But, aside from these fundamentals, some in Moscow apparently did see parallels between free association and the relationship that could evolve between Moscow and the Baltic states.

Soviet officials and regional specialists in Moscow's foreign policy institutes confirmed to the author in mid-1990 that traditional Soviet objectives conflicting with Western interests (for example, political denial of U.S. Navy regional port access and erosion of Australia's commitment to ANZUS) remained on the Soviet agenda. But, it was asserted, these were now subordinate to the new higher priority objectives previously cited. The specialists also claimed that these now-subordinated objectives would be pursued only through "normal diplomatic means." An Australian expert nonetheless notes that, as of 1989, there was no evidence that the Soviets had abandoned extradiplomatic methods of political penetration and manipulation through "nonpolitical" activities such as trade, scientific, cultural, and sporting links and, of course, those of fronts and surrogates.[87]

It is abundantly clear that Moscow's direct pursuit of its objectives in the Pacific islands was marked more by failure than by success. The Soviets offered little in the way of aid or trade of interest to the region, failed to win over any government, and retained a lower level of presence, dialogue, and influence there than in any other global region. Such gains as were made must be measured against the recent zero base. Most political gains, such as those relative to regional nuclear concerns, can be attributed more to indigenous concerns and Australian and New Zealand leftists and peace groups than to Soviet diplomacy or ideology.

Occasional Western inattention to regional concerns and policies in conflict with those of regional states also were major factors in Soviet successes. The old Soviet Union might have wished to continue to seek advantage from such Western weaknesses and pursue low-cost, low-risk opportunities to erode Western influence. Australian Foreign Minister Gareth Evans in December 1989 summed up that concern.

> In the South Pacific, we should expect continued mani-
> festations (for the most part opportunistic) of Soviet
> attempts to gain influence and supporters and to erode
> the strong pro-Western bias of the region, particularly
> since the investment of relatively small resources can
> yield disproportionate results.[88]

Although the Soviet threat in the Pacific islands by the time the Soviet Union ended was at its lowest level since the mid-1970s, uncertainty about the durability of Soviet political and foreign policy reform had justified the concern of the West and the Pacific islands.

9

U.S. Policy: Recommendations and Conclusions

U.S. interests and related objectives in the Pacific islands generally are modest, but some are important. Although the region remains a low-threat environment, challenges to those interests do exist. Some flow or could be resumed from new external influences, but most are intrinsic to the region. Another challenge is of Washington's own making: a proclivity for inattention interspersed with reactive diplomacy. The consequences have been flawed policies or poor policy implementation; a regional perception of U.S. insensitivity toward regional interests and concerns; and a related perception that U.S. policy too often offers more rhetoric than substance. These views are supported by considerable hard evidence.

Although the United States can never fully satisfy regional expectations, there surely is a middle ground between what is hoped for and the inadequacy of current policies. That middle ground can be the place to meet genuine regional needs in ways that further U.S. interests and objectives. Any effort to reach that middle ground must take into account the following interrelated factors:

• The collapse of the Soviet Union, positive shifts in Russian foreign policy, the end of the cold war, and a submerged threat of East-West conflict are all reality. But also real is continuing uncertainty about whether reform on the Russian style will endure. Further, as post–World War II history so abundantly demonstrates, regional threats and conflict having little or no relationship to East-West competition can emerge and threaten U.S. and allied interests.

• The foregoing means that Western strategies to deter conflict will remain relevant at regional and global levels although, fortunately, at lower and less threatening armament levels. Traditional U.S. and other Western strategic interests in the Pacific islands thus will remain relevant, if only because of their relationship to security and other interests in the broader Asia-Pacific area.

• In the emerging new world order, U.S. interests would be well served by recognizing the uniqueness of the Pacific islands region. It is one of the few Third World regions to fully share and practice Western democratic values and to give practical recognition to human rights. Fiji became an aberration, but a temporary one, it is hoped. Successful evolution of the political status of New Caledonia, French Polynesia, and Palau will eliminate the only significant exceptions to self-government or independence. Even with these exceptions, the region is blessed with an absence of single-party repressive dictatorial regimes and has no Marxist or other controlled economies. The island states' ability to sustain this enviable record, however, depends upon whether they can service the legitimate expectations of their people, a requirement to which the United States can and must give more than lip service. It would be a tragic miscalculation to focus exclusively on the problems of emerging democracies elsewhere and, through inattention, contribute to the erosion of those struggling to survive in the Pacific.

• Through historical evolution of their respective links to the Pacific islands, an informal division of labor has emerged among Australia, New Zealand, and the United States. The latter has given primary attention to the Micronesian islands north of the equator, while Australia and

New Zealand have played the lead Western role in the non-
French areas of the South Pacific. Yet most challenges to
U.S. interests are in the South Pacific. It would be impractical and politically unwise to attempt to match or displace
the role of Australia and New Zealand in that subregion,
but a more active U.S. secondary role would well serve
shared interests.

• In refining U.S. policy and related activity in the Pacific islands, it is important to avoid the perception of policy and diplomacy that reacts only to threats to security
interests. Such reactive diplomacy, aside from seldom being
cost-effective, indicates that the United States fails to adequately recognize that most threats to U.S. interests are a
product of the region's political and economic environment
or of U.S. neglect of the region. Most threats have not been
the consequence of Moscow conspiracies. U.S. interests
would be best served by a modest, steady expansion of the
U.S. role in the region in ways that promote regional development, political stability, the strengthening of democratic
institutions, and dialogue with the United States – and that
do not emphasize security over political interests. The two
sets of interests are in fact thoroughly entwined, but the
former are best served by a broad, long-term political strategy. Formulating that strategy requires that the following
issues be addressed comprehensively.

Diplomatic Representation and Dialogue

The United States in the past few years has increased its
regional diplomatic presence and now has four embassies in
the South Pacific (Fiji, Papua New Guinea, Solomon Islands, and Western Samoa) and two in the North Pacific
islands (Federated States of Micronesia and the Marshall
Islands). A small Department of State office in Palau will
become an embassy on implementation of a free association
relationship with the United States.

Resource restraints and cost-effectiveness make impractical the opening of embassies in all regional states. The establishment of one-officer "mini" embassies in the Solomon Islands and Western Samoa, however, has contributed enormously to U.S. relationships with and interests in these states, at a cost of only about $200,000 each annually. This suggests that the United States can respond effectively to Vanuatu's request for an embassy. Given Vanuatu's influential role in Melanesian state affairs, it is important to encourage the new moderate directions of that island state.

Effective management of relations with the seven island states where there are no U.S. embassies requires enough staffing and travel funds at existing embassies to permit frequent travel to those states. In island cultures, face-to-face communication and personal relationships are essential elements of diplomacy. U.S. embassies within the region currently have inadequate staff and resources to satisfy that objective.

For a long time, Washington-based officials seldom visited island states other than Fiji and Papua New Guinea. Fortunately, that pattern is changing at an accelerating pace. Similarly, before 1989 only one South Pacific head of government (Fiji's prime minister in 1984) had ever met with a U.S. president. The Bush administration dramatically altered that pattern. Although it is unrealistic to expect frequent summit meetings between U.S. presidents and their Pacific islands counterparts, they are easy to arrange in Honolulu and might be held when the president is in Hawaii for other purposes. Occasional bilateral meetings must become normal practice.

Of particular importance, the United States must take full advantage of the opportunity offered by the South Pacific Forum heads of government to meet with them annually, on the pattern of the ASEAN postministerial meetings. The United States must be represented by a senior representative knowledgeable about global and regional concerns of South Pacific Forum members. Such representation requires participation at least at the assistant secretary of state level. To ensure the highest possible U.S. representation, the forum should be urged to time its annual meetings to coincide with those of the ASEAN post-ministerial meetings and the annual Australian-U.S. ministerial meetings. The secretary of state would then already be in the region; either he or a senior member of his delegation could attend the forum dialogue meeting at the conclusion of the other two regional events.

Public Diplomacy and Educational and Cultural Exchanges

A generation of South Pacific political leaders and other elites is emerging that has had little or no contact with the United States. Paul Gardner, a recent U.S. ambassador to Papua New Guinea, has pointed out that during much of his tenure, none of the twenty-three members of that country's cabinet had any part of their education in the United States and that neither the prime minister nor the foreign minister had ever visited the United States. In neighboring Vanuatu, only one of the several hundred nationals enrolled in foreign universities was in the United States; few government ministers or officials had ever visited it.[89] Parallel situations exist in some other South Pacific states. The consequences are obvious; images of the United States are based less on reality than on perceptions too often generated by anti-U.S. influences in regional universities and some elements of the region's media. This problem must be addressed at several levels.

U.S. Information Agency international visitor programs that fund travel to and consultations in the United States by island political, labor, academic, and media leaders and other elites should be expanded. Equally, programs (AMPART grants) providing for regional lecture tours by Americans expert on global and regional issues and U.S. foreign policy should be expanded. These are an essential element of public diplomacy.

Undergraduate education and short-term technical training programs for Pacific islanders at the University of Hawaii should be sponsored by the East-West Center, and if possible extended to mainland American universities. Similar programs in the 1960s and early 1970s demonstrated the effectiveness of this kind of educational exchange. Although the Fulbright program normally services postgraduate studies in the United States, grants should be made available to Pacific islanders for one- or two-year undergraduate programs, including associate arts degrees. Fulbright and other programs that provide opportunities for American academics to serve on the faculties of regional universities should also be expanded.

The educational and cultural exchange initiatives announced by President Bush at the 1990 summit meeting in Honolulu are sound steps toward achieving these recommendations.

The Foreign Service Institute of the Department of State has established a training program for diplomats from the Micronesian states in free association with the United States. This program should be expanded to include trainees from the diplomatic services of South Pacific island states. Similar programs in Australia have well served both Australian and island state interests.

U.S. Development Assistance

The level of U.S. development assistance to South Pacific states bears little relationship to U.S. regional interests or to regional expectations and the needs of supportive and democratic friends of the United States. Although there was a modest increase in 1988, current levels are declining. Excluding the $10 million fisheries treaty component of U.S. development assistance, current aid to the South Pacific is less than 1 percent of total regional aid receipts.

As elsewhere, U.S. objectives in providing development assistance are a mix of altruism and the pursuit of U.S.

interests. Department of State–defined development assistance objectives in 1989 included

- maintenance of access to the region's sea-lanes
- assistance to friendly governments that pursue policies supportive of U.S. interests both in the region and in international forums
- restoration and preservation of the regional goodwill toward the United States that has suffered from the lack of U.S. presence in the post–World War II period
- preservation of U.S. access to marine resources in the region's exclusive economic zones
- encouragement of the return of a constitutional representative government in Fiji
- the limiting of Soviet influence in the South Pacific
- continued access to the region's ports for U.S. warships and aircraft.[90]

These objectives, by any measure, showed an ambitious range for an aid program that is one of the smallest anywhere. The issue of how much is enough from the perspectives of either desired political impact or regional expectations and needs can never be satisfactorily quantified. It would seem, however, that incremental increases during the next five years to annual development assistance levels in the range of $30 million to $40 million would be appropriate and could be achieved by fine-tuning global allocations rather than by increasing appropriations. Even at that level, U.S. development assistance would remain well below 10 percent of total flows and far less than that of Australia and Japan. The temptation to cut South Pacific programs and transfer funds to major priorities elsewhere must be resisted. The increase would be insignificant to those priorities, but cuts in South Pacific programs would cause damage out of all proportion to their size.

The U.S. government should also adopt the Australian and New Zealand practice of providing a discretionary aid fund ($50,000 to $100,000) to each embassy in the region.

Careful use of these funds for small projects can have greater political impact than much larger but less visible projects.

The issue of the states' capacity to absorb aid is real, but it can be addressed by funding projects that include contract staff support (to minimize dependence on small island state bureaucracies) and by funding projects that strengthen island state management and other human resources.

Policy Dialogue with Australia, France, Japan, and New Zealand

Policy coordination with Australia, New Zealand, France, and Japan requires strengthening. Consultative processes are excellent only with Australia, and coordination of (as opposed to consultation on) regional policy and policy implementation regarding challenges to shared interests and objectives is nearly nonexistent. Efforts at policy coordination in the past dealt primarily with Soviet regional initiatives. The first step toward broader coordination of Australian, New Zealand, and U.S. policies was the initiation in the early 1980s of annual ANZUS officials' talks on regional matters. One of the unfortunate side effects of the suspension of the ANZUS alliance relationship with New Zealand was the termination of these trilateral consultations. U.S. and other Western interests would be well served by quiet restoration of that consultation process, as well as by their periodic inclusion of France and Japan.

France's regional policies and activities significantly affect all Western interests in the region and thus warrant serious effort to influence their directions. Similarly, Japan's emerging role as a major source of both development assistance and private investment capital ensures that nation new levels of political influence. Consequently, Tokyo must be more thoroughly integrated into Western consultative processes.

Given regional sensitivities often verging on paranoia

vis-à-vis past Western consultative efforts (that is, a perception of conspiracy rather than of consultation), it is important to develop these processes in a quiet, low-key fashion.

Relations with New Zealand

There is no immediate prospect that New Zealand will reverse the antinuclear policies that undercut the United States–New Zealand leg of the ANZUS alliance. Setting aside the ANZUS rift, however, the United States and New Zealand have shared strategic and political interests in the Pacific islands. New Zealand also has considerable influence in some areas of the South Pacific (especially Polynesia), and its defense forces could be a valued Western asset in some regional contingencies. For these reasons, any New Zealand tendencies toward pacifism and isolationism must concern Australia and the United States. A related decline in New Zealand defense force capabilities, resulting in part from termination of ANZUS defense cooperation, but also from inadequate government and public support, also is worrisome.

The United States must demonstrate to other alliance partners that alliance relationships are indeed mutual security arrangements with mutual obligations; an ally cannot ban the U.S. Navy and retain all the benefits of an alliance relationship, particularly in a maritime environment. U.S. suspension of defense obligations to New Zealand, and the subsequent termination of alliance-related cooperation, was necessary, if only for effect elsewhere.

It is nonetheless questionable whether U.S. interests were served by terminating most high-level diplomatic dialogue, particularly when that policy constraint went beyond those constraints in effect for adversaries and did not apply to any other nonallied friends. Restoring contact between the U.S. secretary of state and the New Zealand foreign minister in early 1990 thus was a positive development, which happily has been enlarged upon since then.

Equally, it does not serve U.S. interests to place restraints on defense cooperation (for example, transfers of defense technology and doctrine) that inhibit Australian and New Zealand forces from working together and jointly responding to regional contingencies. Neither does it serve U.S. interests to withhold intelligence relating to shared regional interests. Rigid application of U.S. restraints in these areas can accelerate New Zealand's drift toward pacifism and isolationism and the decay in New Zealand's defense forces.

The defeat of New Zealand's Labor government in late 1990 and its replacement by a National Party government provided opportunities for adjustments in the above policy areas. Although the new government is continuing New Zealand's nuclear-free policies, it seeks closer cooperation with the United States in other areas. If nothing else, it is being more civil and constructive in the way it communicates with Washington.

The Russian Challenge

A regional challenge for the West will be to develop a political strategy that channels a Russian regional presence in directions that help integrate the successor to the Soviet Union into normal global political and economic processes. That effort also will serve some of Moscow's legitimate new regional and global priorities and will provide Russia a vested interest in regional stability.

As a practical matter, however, that objective has limited potential in the Pacific islands. Aside from fisheries access, opportunities for new economic relationships are few. Development of even these limited opportunities, as elsewhere, will depend heavily on Russian success in moving toward a competitive market economy, including ruble convertibility.

Russian membership in most Pacific islands regional organizations is an unrealistic objective. Even the United

States, with its Pacific islands territorial presence, qualifies for full membership in only one major regional organization, the South Pacific Commission.

The development of effective strategies to deal with the Russians in the Pacific islands will in very great measure depend upon consultations with Canberra and Wellington, but also Tokyo, Paris, and, above all, regional state governments. This might best be done through the annual post–South Pacific Forum meeting dialogue. Ideally, the parameters of acceptable and indeed welcome Russian regional activities would be identified and conveyed as appropriate or necessary to Moscow. Such activities would include normal diplomatic activity, fisheries access, and trade. The cost of potential political meddling or other inappropriate activities should be made clear. Given the level of Australia's South Pacific interests and the high priority Moscow attaches to its relations with Australia, Canberra might take the lead in discussions related to the South Pacific, as the United States should for the North Pacific islands.

The possibility of Russian interest in operating through regional organizations with respect to any future regional aid projects, and a possible interest in shifting from bilateral fisheries agreements to a regional agreement, should be encouraged. Regional organizations are far better equipped to negotiate and monitor such arrangements than are most island state governments.

One major area of potential cooperation for Russia, the regional states, and some Western powers is that of marine resource–related oceanographic and hydrographic research. There should be cooperation with island state governments and regional organizations on necessary political and technical safeguards. Joint ventures involving exchanges of Western and Russian data relevant to future seabed mining might also be explored.

Finally, existing Australian, New Zealand, and U.S. intelligence cooperation with island state governments should be conducted in normal fashion as an effort to strengthen the latter's capabilities to deal with Russian initiatives. Cooperation might be expanded in intelligence and security training relevant to an "on the ground" Russian presence, even if that presence is in the foreseeable future likely to be benign.

Cooperation with Regional Organizations

As discussed in chapter 2, the region is unique with respect to the development and success of regional organizations that service the political, economic, and social needs of their members. The effectiveness of these institutions, but particularly the South Pacific Forum, the South Pacific Commission, and the Forum Fisheries Agency, is very much in the U.S. interest, given their contributions to the development of the region and therefore to regional stability. The tendency of island cultures to resolve issues through consensus rather than confrontation also ensures that regional organizations, in addressing controversial issues, generally adopt moderate and pragmatic courses of action.

The issues involved for the United States are relatively few, but important. The continuing existence of the South Pacific Commission is in the U.S. interest. It is the only major regionwide organization of which the United States is a member and the only one that provides an equal regional voice for dependent territories. It also is one of the few remaining links between the region and Great Britain.

The United States thus should continue to oppose initiatives that would replace the commission with a single regional organization that would exclude the United States, Great Britain, France, and the region's dependent territories. Strategies essential to the preservation of the commission must include competent U.S. representation at commission meetings. Designating representatives with no knowledge of and little interest in the region ill serves U.S. interests.

Of particular importance, the United States must pay arrearages in assessed contributions. It is a major embarrassment when the world's richest nation does not meet its legal obligations in the world's poorest region. Although not a fully satisfactory resolution of this issue, Congress in late 1990 did authorize payment of these and all other international organization arrearages over the following five years at 20 percent per year.

The Environment

Global Warming and the Greenhouse Effect

Concerns about global warming and the greenhouse effect now parallel and to some degree exceed the nuclear issue in terms of emotional and long-term political impact. If industrial states do not take major corrective action, regional governments assume that all island states may suffer unique levels of devastation and, in some cases, may disappear. The magnitude of the U.S. contribution to global warming (currently 22 percent of carbon dioxide emissions), coupled with a current U.S. ambivalence toward adopting remedial measures other than research, makes it very likely this issue will increasingly plague U.S. relations in this region. It is not an issue that can be resolved in the context of U.S. Pacific islands policies and U.S. relations in that region. But it is important to understand the impact of the issue on these relationships. It may be that no amount of "good" policy in other issue areas can undo the damage done by present U.S. attitudes and inaction on global warming.

The South Pacific Nuclear Free Zone

Although the trade-offs involved are difficult to assess accurately, the United States should periodically and objectively review its position on signing and ratifying the SPNFZ treaty protocols. It is generally accepted that adherence would not hurt U.S. security interests and requirements in the South Pacific but would well serve regional political interests.

The major remaining issue is whether adherence would in fact significantly strengthen pressure for nuclear-weapons-free zones in other, more strategically critical regions, which could damage U.S. security interests in those areas. Many would argue that each region will move toward such zones on the basis of regional political and security imperatives and not because of the precedent set by U.S. adherence to a nuclear-free zone in the South Pacific or, for that matter, the example already set by the Treaty of Tlatelolco for Latin America.

Should the United States decide to sign the SPNFZ protocols, a related issue will be the question of extending the South Pacific Nuclear Free Zone to the Marshall Islands, Federated States of Micronesia, and Palau. Each almost certainly would seek to become treaty signatories. Each probably could not do so if the United States did not agree that such action would be consistent with U.S. defense responsibilities as defined by the free association compacts. Adhering to the treaty would prohibit the states from stationing and storing nuclear weapons within their jurisdictions, but it would not affect U.S. Navy port access or transits of U.S. aircraft, nuclear-armed or not. The 1991 U.S. decision to remove tactical nuclear weapons from naval and air assets should help clear the way for changed U.S. policy.

As a practical matter, the United States has already agreed with Palau, the most strategically significant of the three, that it will not station or store nuclear weapons in Palau in a free association relationship. No U.S. military facilities exist in or are contemplated for the Federated States, and none are contemplated for the Marshalls beyond the existing Kwajalein Missile Range facility, which involves no stationing or storage of nuclear weaponry. Peacetime nuclear weapon storage and stationing are prohibited by the free association compacts with the latter two states. It is difficult to conceive of any Pacific contingencies that would require any change in that regard. Any future U.S. adherence to the SPNFZ protocols consequently should be paralleled by acceptance of Micronesian state SPNFZ treaty adherence.

A further consideration is France's potential reaction to U.S. adherence. The United States has attached importance to an independent French nuclear deterrent and agreed that such a capability requires testing. (Past U.S. efforts to resolve the testing-site issue by offering use of the Nevada nuclear test site to France on the same basis as British use have been rejected by Paris as incompatible with an independent capability.) The French government asserted in consultations with Washington in 1986 and 1987 that U.S. signing of the SPNFZ protocols would damage Franco-U.S. defense cooperation.

France, however, more than most nations, practices the principle of acting on the requirements of its regional interests, even when they conflict with those of allies. That principle suggests that Paris would initially react to U.S. adherence with annoyance but would quickly accept it. France's decision to place nuclear testing in abeyance at least through 1992 is a hopeful sign.

In considering these issues, it is important to remember that signing and ratifying the SPNFZ protocols would commit the United States only to refrain from nuclear testing within the zone (not an issue), from stationing and storing nuclear weapons in American Samoa (not a serious issue), from using nuclear weapons against zone states (most certainly not an issue), and from assisting those that test within the zone (a possible concern vis-à-vis any sharing of nuclear test technology with France). Adherence does not commit the signatory to prevent others from testing. An argument against adherence, sometimes voiced by U.S. officials ignorant of regional state policies and SPNFZ restraints, is that such action would preclude stationing of nuclear weaponry in Australia or other zone states. That assertion ignores the fact that all zone states already have national policies prohibiting storage or stationing of nuclear weaponry on their territory and that SPNFZ has codified these national policies.

Other Environmental Issues

The U.S. case for destroying chemical weaponry on Johnston Atoll, including that previously stored in Germany, is excellent. That most U.S. chemical weapons will be destroyed at similar facilities within the United States responds effectively to the concern that Pacific islands have been singled out for a unique risk.

There is now resigned tolerance of the Johnston Atoll project by most regional state governments. But that tolerance is based on President Bush's personal assurance that Johnston Atoll will not be used to destroy more chemical weapons after its current assigned tasks are completed and that it will not be used as a dump site for other toxic wastes. Any breach of that commitment would be devastating on U.S. credibility within the region.

The Johnston Atoll situation offers yet another lesson. The U.S. government did make a major effort to brief regional governments on the project, but only after Greenpeace and other environmental groups had made it a major regional concern and issue. There apparently was little effort to brief regional governments or the regional media beforehand. If there had been a serious effort, it is likely that the issue never would have reached the proportions it did. Given the history of regional concern about dumping toxic wastes, nuclear testing, and other environmental issues, the failure to provide adequate advance briefings and consultations represents inexcusable diplomatic insensitivity and a painful lesson for future controversial U.S. regional initiatives.

Marine Resources

Jurisdictional differences over tuna that led to a crisis in U.S. relations with the region were mooted by the 1987 regional fisheries treaty and eliminated by U.S. legislation in 1990. The latter now makes bilateral fisheries agreements possible. The regional treaty, however, is demonstrably the single most important and positive U.S. diplomatic initiative in recent years. It has been well received in the region, within Congress, and even by the U.S. tuna industry. It almost certainly is more cost effective than multiple bilateral arrangements. Congress has called for negotiation of a ten-year extension of the five-year treaty, and the president made a personal commitment at the 1990 Honolulu summit to commence that negotiation soon. Fulfilling that commitment promptly is essential to U.S. credibility within the region.

Trade and Investment

All island states prefer development through private foreign investment and export trade opportunities instead of aid handouts. President Bush's 1990 summit initiatives in the area of promoting U.S. investment in and trade with the Pacific islands were thus well received by island heads of government. Again, however, U.S. credibility is at stake, and adequate governmental and private sector followup will be critical. It will be especially important to institutionalize effectively these initiatives through the Joint Commercial Commission. This process should include assigning to the South Pacific (Port Moresby and Suva) Department of Commerce Foreign Commercial Service officers who can service the region—for example, by communicating with the South Pacific Forum Secretariat and coordinating Commercial Commission activities. Their presence over time would eliminate a major obstacle to U.S. investment in and trade with the region—that is, U.S. private-sector lack of awareness of opportunities.

Consideration should also be given to nonreciprocal free-trade arrangements with the Pacific islands similar to aspects of the U.S. Caribbean Initiative and Australian and New Zealand arrangements with the Pacific islands (the South Pacific Regional Trade and Economic Cooperation

Agreement – SPARTECA) that provide for tariff-free entry of island state products. Free entry of Pacific islands products into the United States would have almost no impact on U.S. industry but would provide an important market and major incentive to small industry in the Pacific islands. The political impact of such an arrangement would be highly significant.

The Future of New Caledonia

Although it is difficult to see an effective practical role for the United States, measures (even if only symbolic) that support efforts to peacefully resolve New Caledonia's political future should be explored. The United States should also recognize that the Kanaks are likely to achieve the independence or autonomy they seek. This likelihood requires cultivation of the leadership of that community. Kanak expressions of interest in U.S. educational opportunities and private-sector investment in New Caledonia should be explored and acted upon.

Palau and the Micronesian States

Continuing uncertainty about the political future of Palau brings into question the viability of limited U.S. defense options in those islands and is a regional political embarrassment. Although Palauans themselves must resolve Palauan constitutional issues blocking resolution of their political future, the United States should encourage and support that effort by all appropriate means. For one thing, the United States should review its defense options in Palau. Are they in fact necessary? Alternatives to free association, including independence, should also be explored – if Palau desires that course. Any arrangement, however, that provides for U.S. defense responsibility must at a minimum allow routine U.S. naval and air access, including by ships and aircraft that may be nuclear-armed and by ships that are nuclear-propelled.

Meanwhile, the Department of the Interior decision to reimpose internal administrative authority over Palau – after nine years of self-government – may be highly counterproductive vis-à-vis broader U.S. political objectives in these islands. The action could reinforce existing hostility toward the United States; it might also erode the existing majority support for continuing political relations. This new issue also diverts attention from the fundamental question of Palau's post-trusteeship status. The Interior Department should reverse course.

The United States also should make a major public diplomacy effort in Australia, New Zealand, and the Pacific islands to counter distortions of the situation within Palau and of the U.S. position on Palau's future.

U.S. relations with the Federated States of Micronesia and the Marshall Islands are evolving well. The extension of U.S. domestic federal services to these states, however, is inappropriate to their relation with the United States. (Some Micronesians have pointed out that their islands are the only sovereign foreign states with a U.S. postal Zip Code!) These programs also provide considerable potential for bilateral friction. Most should be phased out as rapidly as they can be replaced by Micronesian counterparts.

Micronesian state efforts to diversify and reduce their economic dependence through development assistance and private-sector investment from Japan, Australia, and other friendly or allied nations should continue to be encouraged. Multiple links with governments that have security and other interests shared with the United States operate to U.S. advantage.

International recognition and acceptance of the Micronesian states have proceeded reasonably well in the Pacific area, including through their participation in the South Pacific Forum and other key regional organizations. Australia, Japan, New Zealand, the People's Republic of China, the Philippines, and the other island states have established diplomatic relations with them. With the trusteeship agreement termination now resolved, the United States undoubtedly will encourage U.S. friends and allies elsewhere, especially in Asia and Europe, to take similar action. Of critical practical importance, the two states must also be given every assistance in their efforts to gain membership in the UN specialized agencies and other international organizations. The same applies with respect to their accession to the Vienna consular and diplomatic conventions and other important international treaty regimes. The EC should be urged to extend the Lome Convention and its aid and trade programs to the two states. (Although access to Lome Convention programs is mainly by former European colonies, there are numerous exceptions. The latter usually are based on distant past colonial ties—for example, those of Haiti with France and those of Western Samoa with Germany. The Micronesian states in free association with the United States would qualify for this kind of exception because of historical Spanish and German links.)

At some point the Micronesian states may seek UN membership. Given the U.S. position that the two states are sovereign and responsible for their foreign affairs, Washington should raise no obstacles. This may require some adjustment of State Department positions. The State Department has asserted that UN membership may be inconsistent with the provisions of the free association compact that vests defense responsibility in the United States: the Micronesian governments might take positions in the UN that conflict with that responsibility. This line of legal reasoning is flawed. Other compact provisions require that the Micronesian governments take no action that is incompatible with U.S. defense responsibilities. In conducting their foreign affairs, they are obligated to consult with the United States, and the latter has full authority to determine what constitutes a conflict with its defense responsibilities.

Any U.S. effort to block UN membership, if it is sought by these two states, could have a devastating impact on U.S. interests in and relations with them.

The U.S. Territories

Although not yet a significant regional issue, developments in Guam described in chapter 5 require that the character of a future commonwealth relationship with the United States be resolved at an early date. Similarly, an emerging desire in American Samoa for higher levels of self-government should be addressed. Either a commonwealth relationship similar to that of the Northern Marianas or free association would be appropriate. Whatever their future status, the American Samoans probably will seek U.S. citizenship instead of keeping their present "U.S. national" status. They also will insist upon continuing arrangements that protect Samoan lands and culture. These desires should be accommodated.

Pressures on the part of the Northern Marianas for changes in their relationship inconsistent with U.S. sovereignty should be resisted. They should be advised that, if they prefer the benefits of free association to those of commonwealth status, they are welcome to change their status, which would include lowering levels of financial subsidy.

Related to the future of Guam, American Samoa, and the Northern Mariana Islands is the Department of the Interior's territorial management role. A strong case can be made that the department's intensive and intrusive involvement in territorial affairs impedes more than improves the territories' political, economic, and social development. Present arrangements also reflect a level of paternalism that gives little or no recognition to the level of sophistication of territorial governments and their sensitivities. One option would be to phase out Interior Department territorial responsibilities and phase in Washington territorial representation offices that would work with congressional and executive branch agencies on federal grants and programs essential to the territories.

The Department of State should recognize that territorial leaders, particularly those in American Samoa, have influence within the region, that the territories participate

in some regional organizations, and that regional developments and related U.S. policies directly affect the well-being
of the territories. Territorial leaders also have insights with
respect to promoting U.S. interests in the region that are a
valuable but seldom-used asset. The Department of State
should adopt the French practice of institutionalizing territorial involvement in the development and implementation
of regional policies.

Possibilities for terminating the non-self-governing status of the U.S. territories (and thus the decolonization issue)
should be explored. One option would be for each territory
to have a UN-observed act of self-determination with ballot
choices between independence and agreed-upon forms of
commonwealth or other relationships with the United
States. Such a ballot would be a no-risk course for the territories and the United States, put to rest potential external
decolonization pressures, terminate very limited UN jurisdiction, and end the requirement to report annually to the
United Nations on U.S. administration of the territories.

Pacific Islands Policy Management

To ensure an adequate level of policy sensitivity, continuity,
and focus for the entire region, the Department of State
must give higher priority to development and use a corps of
regional specialists, as it does for other regions. Up to 1990,
only three foreign service officers had ever been trained as
Pacific islands area specialists.[91] As of that date, none was
being utilized. The State Department should also make
more frequent effective use of officers who have acquired
experience through regional assignments. The tendency to
staff regional embassies and key positions in Washington
with officers having no relevant experience guarantees in-
advertent insensitivity to regional concerns and flawed policies. The perceived absence of a career track to senior positions dealing with the region also makes it difficult to
recruit and retain regional expertise. There is the accurate

perception within the U.S. Foreign Service that the most
senior regional positions traditionally go either to political
appointees or to career officers from other area specializa-
tions being rewarded for service elsewhere. The same problems exist with respect to management of relations with
Australia and New Zealand.

Yet another problem has been structural. Before 1989,
except for a brief period late in the Carter administration
and early in the Reagan administration, Australia, New
Zealand, and the Pacific islands have been treated as an
adjunct to other and larger regions. Between 1984 and
1989, the deputy assistant secretary of state responsible for
the areas also was responsible for relations with China,
Mongolia, Hong Kong, and Taiwan. No other such "odd
couple" policy-management arrangement exists in the Department of State. Australia, New Zealand, and the Pacific
islands could never really complete for time and attention in
competition with issues involving China. This organization-
al problem was rectified in 1989 by reestablishing a deputy
assistant secretary position responsible for Australian,
New Zealand, and Pacific islands affairs. That arrangement
should become permanent.

There are no easy ways to implement some of the above
recommendations, especially since several require trade-offs
between U.S. regional interests and those elsewhere. On the
other hand, the investment in attention, sensitivity to legitimate regional concerns, and human and financial resources
would be exceptionally modest relative to other regions and
to the potential gain for U.S. interests.

Notes

1. The United States, Australia, and New Zealand have since restored development assistance to Fiji, but not defense cooperation.

2. Grants and other financial subsidies by an administering authority to its dependent territories are not generally defined as "official development assistance." The term normally is applied only to aid received by sovereign states.

3. For a full discussion of U.S. regional security requirements and criteria for adherence to nuclear-weapons-free zones and of the U.S. position on SPNFZ, see U.S. Congress, House Committee on Foreign Affairs, *The South Pacific Nuclear Free Zone, Hearings and Markup before the Committee on Foreign Affairs and Its Subcommittee on Asian and Pacific Affairs on H. Con. Res. 158,* 100th Cong., 1st sess., 1987. Also, U.S. Congress, House Committee on Foreign Affairs, *United States Interests in the South Pacific, Hearing before the Subcommittee on Asian and Pacific Affairs,* 101st Cong., 1st sess., 1989.

4. Ibid.

5. Ibid.

6. Admiral Hays, now retired, confirmed the foregoing to the author in a conversation on August 28, 1989. He replaced Adm. William Crowe, Jr., as CINCPAC in 1986 and served in that position until 1988. Admiral Crowe became chairman of the Joint Chiefs of Staff in 1986.

7. The author witnessed this confusion on several occasions

between 1985 and 1987. It appeared most frequently among senior Department of Defense officials.

8. Ibid.

9. For an example of this theme, see Stewart Firth, *Nuclear Playground* (Sydney: Allen & Unwin Australia Pty. Ltd., 1987).

10. Australian Prime Minister Hawke raised the issue at the highest levels of the U.S. government during his June 1989 official visit to Washington. More recently, at the October 1990 Honolulu summit meeting between President Bush and Pacific islands heads of government, the latter strongly pressed for U.S. adherence. President Bush cited U.S. global security requirements in reaffirming the U.S. position.

11. Among these statements was that of Acting Deputy Assistant Secretary of State Richard Williams in testimony on July 27, 1989, before the Subcommittee on Asia and the Pacific of the Committee on Foreign Affairs, U.S. House of Representatives. He said that the review was nearly complete and that the decision was likely to be nonadherence to the protocols of the Treaty of Rarotonga.

12. For a comprehensive discussion of the New Caledonia issue, see Helen Fraser, *New Caledonia, Anti-Colonialism in a Pacific Territory* (Canberra: Australian National University Press, 1988); and George K. Tanham, *New Caledonia: The Fragile Peace* (Santa Monica, Calif.: The RAND Corporation, 1990). The latter report was prepared for the Department of Defense.

13. Tanham, *New Caledonia: The Fragile Peace,* 21–22.

14. From an unpublished address by Kiribati President Tabai at the September 7, 1986, opening of the Waigani Seminar, University of Papua New Guinea, Port Moresby, Papua New Guinea.

15. For a full discussion of that review, see John C. Dorrance, *Oceania and the United States: An Analysis of U.S. Interests and Policy in the South Pacific* (Washington, D.C.: National Defense University Press, 1980).

16. The absence of any present intent to exercise military options in Palau or in the Northern Mariana Islands was confirmed to the author in 1990 by senior Department of Defense officials and by senior officers at CINCPAC headquarters in Honolulu.

17. Aadu Karemaa, "What Would Mahan Say about Space Power?" *Proceedings of the U.S. Naval Institute,* 114/4/1022

(April 1988), 48–49. For further discussion of this technology, see Michael Richardson, "Why the Russians Are Coming," *Pacific Defense Reporter*, September 1988, p. 11.

18. Australia seized New Guinea and Nauru from Germany, and New Zealand occupied Western Samoa in the same time frame. Each was a League of Nations Mandate between the two world wars. After World War II, they were administered as UN trust territories until independence.

19. E. J. Kahn, Jr., *A Reporter in Micronesia* (New York: W. W. Norton & Company, 1966), 25.

20. Statement quoted in James N. Murray, Jr., *The United Nations Trusteeship System* (Urbana: The University of Illinois Press, 1957), 29.

21. Statement by Ambassador Warren Austin before the UN Security Council. Text quoted in Dorothy Richard, *United States Naval Administration of the Trust Territory of the Pacific Islands*, vol. 3 (Washington, D.C.: Office of the Chief of Naval Operations, U.S. Navy, 1957), 32.

22. The latter was set up in 1951 and closed down in 1962.

23. National Security Action Memorandum 145 of April 18, 1962. Also see U.S. Congress, House Foreign Affairs Committee, *Approving the Compact of Free Association between the United States, the Marshall Islands and the Federated States of Micronesia*, 97th Cong., 1st sess., April 23–24; May 2, 14, 15, 1985, pp. 467–468.

24. Ibid. President Kennedy had commissioned Harvard economist Anthony N. Solomon to lead a study mission on the future of the territory. His "Report by the U.S. Government Survey Mission to the Trust Territory of the Pacific Islands" was submitted to the White House in October 1963. It was in large measure ignored in the aftermath of Kennedy's assassination a few weeks later, perhaps in part because of the White House's increasing preoccupation with Vietnam.

25. Statement by Senate President Amata Kabua, Congress of Micronesia, *Journal of the Senate*, 4th regular session, 2d Congress, August 6, 1968, pp. 444–445.

26. Congress of Micronesia, Future Political Status Commission, *Report to the Congress of Micronesia*, 2d session, 3d Congress, July 1969, p. 8.

27. Walter Hickel, *Who Owns America?* (Englewood Cliffs, N.J.: Prentice-Hall, Inc., 1971), 108. Hickel states that Kissinger

made this remark during a discussion of Micronesian future political status issues. Hickel was President Nixon's secretary of interior at the time of the meeting.

28. Saipan and most of the other Northern Marianas were almost immediately transferred back to the Navy Department in connection with the establishment in 1951 of the CIA base on that island. It remained under navy administration until the early 1960s when it was again transferred to the Interior Department. Shortly afterward, the headquarters of the territory's U.S. administration was transferred from Guam to Saipan – the first time the trust territory was administered from within its own political boundaries!

29. The Northern Marianas government does not accept the U.S. government's view that sovereignty was transferred to or acquired by the United States in 1986. It asserts that the Northern Marianas are sovereign.

30. See table 5 for further data and sources.

31. Compact of Free Association between the United States, the Republic of the Marshall Islands and the Federated States of Micronesia, Title 3, Article 1, section 311.

32. Ibid.

33. Separate and protracted negotiations with the Marshall Islands also led to compensation to Marshallese landowners who had been displaced by nuclear testing at Bikini and Eniwetok atolls and to Marshallese exposed in 1952 to nuclear test fallout occasioned by an unexpected shift in wind directions (the Bravo Test). A $150 million endowment fund provides that compensation.

34. Compact of Free Association between the United States and the Republic of Palau, Title 3, Article 3, section 352.

35. Compact of Free Association between the United States and the Republic of Palau, Title 3, Article 2, section 324.

36. Many of these problems, but especially the latter, are documented in United States General Accounting Office (USGAO), *U.S. Trust Territory – Issues Associated with Palau's Transition to Self-Government* (Washington, D.C.: USGAO, July 1989).

37. Ibid.

38. Pending termination of the trusteeship agreement, the latter has legal precedence over Palau's constitution.

39. U.S., Australian, and New Zealand peace groups have

been particularly active and have generated widespread but distorted TV and print media coverage of Palau throughout the Pacific and Europe.

40. For citations of territorial leadership frustrations with and perceptions of the Office of Territorial Affairs and the Department of the Interior, see *The Washington Pacific Report* 7, no. 13, April 1, 1989, p. 3.

41. For a full discussion of the evolution and implementation of U.S. policy during this period, see Dorrance, *Oceania and the United States: An Analysis*.

42. Statement of Richard Holbrooke, assistant secretary of state for East Asian and Pacific Affairs on July 31, 1978, U.S. Congress, Subcommittee on East Asian and Pacific Affairs, Senate Committee on Foreign Relations, *Emerging Pacific Island Community*, App. A, 95th Cong., 2d sess., 1978.

43. These perceptions were conveyed to the author by a cross section of island political leaders and scholars at various times between 1979 and 1990.

44. As of the end of 1990, the United States was in arrears for approximately $420,000 for dues that were payable in 1986 and 1987. The United States is behind in its dues to nearly all international organizations of which it is a member because of shortfalls in congressional appropriations in those years.

45. Congressman Solarz, chairman of the House Foreign Affairs Subcommittee on Asia and the Pacific, visited the Solomon Islands and other South Pacific states in 1989 and proposed this project in his subsequent report. Apparently he had also promised the Solomon Islands prime minister that he would seek a U.S. appropriation for the project. He also solicited and obtained CINCPAC support. See U.S. Congress, Committee on Foreign Affairs, *Problems in Paradise: United States Interests in the South Pacific, Report of a Congressional Delegation to the South Pacific, August 5-16, 1989*, 101st Cong., 2d sess., 1990, p. 71.

46. As one major example, see Department of State, *Report to Congress Concerning Oceania* (Washington, D.C.: Department of State, 1990). The report, which describes U.S. interests in and policies toward the Pacific islands, was prepared in compliance with Public Law 101-426 (Foreign Relations Authorization Act for FY 1990-1991), sec. 1008, p. 75.

47. For a discussion of the new strategy, see Agency for In-

ternational Development, *Regional Development Strategy Statement, FY 1990-1994* (Suva, Fiji: USAID South Pacific Regional Development Office, 1988).

48. Eleven of the region's thirteen states were represented. The prime ministers of Niue and Vanuatu could not attend because of domestic political problems. Tonga was represented by the monarchy's crown prince, the Solomons by its deputy prime minister. The presidents or prime ministers of the remaining nine states were present.

49. Department of State officers provided details on the meeting to the author. A further source is Floyd Takeuchi, "The Day George Bush Sat Down with the Leaders of the Islands," *Islands Business*, November 1990, pp. 16–17.

50. Ibid.

51. These comments were offered in a public exchange of remarks between President Bush and Prime Minister Henry at the conclusion of the October 27, 1990, summit. Henry served as spokesman for the other Pacific island participants. See "Remarks by Prime Minister Geoffrey Henry of Cook Islands" (Washington, D.C.: White House press release, October 27, 1990).

52. "U.S. Vows to Honour Australian Defence Deal," *Sydney Morning Herald*, June 26, 1989, p. 8. Also, "Trade Problems No Bar to Alliance," *Sydney Daily Telegraph*, June 26, 1989, p. 12.

53. From a speech by the Honorable Rawdon Dalrymple, Australian ambassador to the United States, before the Asia Society, New York, September 25, 1985.

54. The bombing, which sank the *Rainbow Warrior* and killed a crew member, blocked that vessel's intended protest voyage to the French nuclear test site at Moruroa Atoll in French Polynesia. Two of the French agents involved were arrested, tried, and convicted by the New Zealand government. They were subsequently transferred to French custody but have since been released by the French government.

55. John Hoffman, "Second Walkout by Soviet Bloc Envoys," *Sydney Morning Herald*, June 13, 1978, p. 32.

56. Hua Di, "The Soviet Threat to the Northern Pacific Region from an Overall Point of View," *Atlantic Community Quarterly* 24, Spring 1986, pp. 145–149.

57. George K. Tanham and Eleanor S. Wainstein, *Papua New Guinea Today* (Santa Monica, Calif.: The RAND Corporation,

1990), 34. This report was prepared for the under secretary of defense for policy, Department of Defense.

58. Tanham, *New Caledonia: The Fragile Peace*, 11.

59. Much of the data and analysis in this chapter, including the descriptions of Soviet interest, objectives, activities, and policies, was either confirmed or obtained in meetings with Soviet officials and academic regional specialists during a visit to Moscow in mid-1990.

60. Richard F. Staar, *Yearbook on International Communist Affairs, 1990* (Stanford, Calif.: Hoover Institution Press, 1990), 274.

61. U.S. Information Agency (USIA), *Wireless File* (Washington, D.C.: USIA, September 10, 1986).

62. David Hegarty, "The Soviet Union in the South Pacific in the 1990s," *The Soviets in the Pacific in the 1990s*, edited by Ross Babbage (Sydney: Brassey's Australia, 1989), 115–116 and 124–125.

63. Ibid, 118.

64. Giff Johnson, "Soviet Talks of Trade for Micronesia, Yes," *Islands Business*, November 1990, p. 52. The foregoing reports an interview with Dr. Viktor Vrevsky during his October 1990 visits to Guam, Palau, and the Federated States of Micronesia. Vrevsky is chairman, Department of South Pacific Studies, Institute of Oriental Studies, Soviet Academy of Sciences. He served as a consultant to the Soviet Foreign Ministry.

65. Robin Bromby, "Getting Caught in a Tuna Treaty," *Pacific Islands Monthly*, October 1990, p. 23.

66. Ibid, 120.

67. Department of State, *Soviet Influence Activities: A Report on Active Measures and Propaganda, 1987–1988* (Washington, D.C.: Department of State, 1989).

68. For a recent example, see "Palau Votes to Decide on U.S. Compact," Moscow TASS in English, February 6, 1990. Cited in FBIS-SOV-90-026, February 7, 1990, p. 21.

69. That assertion may be less than credible. The Soviet Union mounted major new disinformation programs elsewhere as recently as in 1989 and 1990 – especially in the Philippines.

70. Johnson, "Soviet Talks of Trade for Micronesia, Yes."

71. For an excellent overview of Soviet surrogate activity, see George Tanham, "Subverting the South Pacific," *The National*

Interest 11, Spring 1988, pp. 85–94. For details on related trade union activity, see Michael Easson, "Labor and the Left in the Pacific," *The Red Orchestra*, edited by Dennis Bark and Owen Harries (Stanford, Calif.: Hoover Institution Press, 1989). I have drawn heavily on these sources.

72. A small Fiji union affiliated with the WFTU in the early 1980s. That affiliation has since been terminated.

73. Michael Easson is secretary of the New South Wales Labor Council in Australia. He made these points in conversations with the author between 1985 and 1989. Also, see Easson, "Labor and the Left in the Pacific."

74. Ibid.

75. Tanham, "Subverting the South Pacific," 94.

76. Data on the Soviet military buildup and capabilities are drawn primarily from Department of Defense, *Soviet Military Power: Prospects for Change, 1989* (Washington, D.C.: Department of Defense, 1989).

77. The U.S. position on Pacific naval arms control issues was under review in Washington at the end of 1990.

78. Hegarty, "The Soviet Union in the South Pacific in the 1990s," 117.

79. "Gorbachev *Merdeka* Interview: 'Global Double Zero' for Medium-Range Missiles," *Summary of World Broadcasts*, SU/8628/A3/1–9, July 24, 1987, p. 5.

80. This point was informally confirmed to the author on several occasions in 1990 by senior officials of the departments of Defense and State.

81. The Soviet deputy representative to the UN Security Council, Valintin V. Lozinskiy, described these assurances in a statement to the council on December 22, 1990. See Paul Lewis, "Soviets Yield to U.S. on Pacific Islands' Status," *New York Times*, December 24, 1990, p. 5.

82. Interview with Vice Admiral Dmitry Komarov reported in *The Australian* newspaper, March 21, 1988, p. 13.

83. Hegarty, "The Soviet Union in the South Pacific in the 1990s," 122–123.

84. Author's conversations with Soviet officials and academic regional specialists in Moscow in mid-1990.

85. Johnson, "Soviet Talks of Trade for Micronesia, Yes," 52.

86. "Gorbachev: France Also Didn't Grant Independence Overnight," *Washington Post*, June 4, 1990, p. A18.

87. Hegarty, "The Soviet Union in the South Pacific in the 1990s," 120.

88. Senator Gareth Evans, minister for foreign affairs and trade, "Australia's Regional Security," ministerial statement released by the Department of Foreign Affairs and Trade, Canberra, Australia, December 6, 1989, p. 5.

89. Author's conversation with Paul Gardner in 1989.

90. Statement of William Clark, Jr., acting assistant secretary of state for East Asian and Pacific affairs, before the Subcommittee on Asian and Pacific Affairs, House Foreign Affairs Committee, U.S. House of Representatives, February 27, 1989. See Department of State, "FY 1990 Foreign Assistance Requests for East Asia and the Pacific," *Current Policy No. 1190* (Washington, D.C.: Bureau of Public Affairs, Department of State, February 27, 1989), 3–4.

91. A fourth officer, who had previously served at the U.S. embassy in the Federated States of Micronesia, was assigned to Pacific islands area specialization training in late 1990.

Index